Fables of a Jewish Aesop

D1523216

Fables
of a Jewish Aesop

Translated from the Fox Fables
of Berechiah ha-Nakdan by

MOSES HADAS

Illustrated with woodcuts by

FRITZ KREDEL

Preface by

DAVID HADAS

NONPAREIL BOOKS

David R. Godine, Publisher

BOSTON

This is a *Nonpareil Book*
first published in 2001 by
DAVID R. GODINE, PUBLISHER
Post Office Box 450
Jaffrey, New Hampshire 03452
www.godine.com

LIBRARY OF CONGRESS
CATALOGING-IN-PUBLICATION DATA
Berechiah ben Natronai ha-Nakdan, 12th/13th cent.
[Mishle shu'alim. English]
Fables of a Jewish Aesop /
translated from the Fox Fables of
Berechiah ha-Nakdan by Moses Hadas ;
foreword by David Hadas ;
illustrated with woodcuts by Fritz Kredel.
p. cm.
Originally published: New York:
Columbia University Press, 1967
ISBN 1-56792-131-0 (softcover : alk paper)
1. Fables, Hebrew. I. Kredel, Fritz, 1900-1973.
II. Title.
PJ5050.B4 M513 2000
398.24'5'089924–dc21 00-035425

First Printing
Printed in the United States of America

Contents

	Preface by David Hadas	*ix*
	Introduction by W. T. H. Jackson	*xiii*
	Author's Proem	*1*
1	Lion, Beasts, Cattle	*7*
2	Mouse, Frog, Eagle	*9*
3	Wolf & Sheep at the River	*12*
4	Cock & Gem	*13*
5	Dog, Cheese, Water	*14*
6	Fox & Fishes	*16*
7	Dog, Sheep, Lion, Wolf, Bear	*18*
8	Wolf & Crane	*20*
9	A Pregnant Bitch & Another	*22*
10	City Mouse & Country Mouse	*25*
11	Fox & Eagle	*27*
12	Lion, Goat, Sheep, Cow	*29*
13	Crow & Fox	*31*
14	Ass, Dog, Man	*32*
15	Lion, Mouse, Snare	*34*
16	Dove & Flax	*36*
17	Cicada & Ant	*38*
18	Raven & Sheep	*40*
19	Two Deer	*41*
20	Eagle, Snail, Raven	*42*
21	Wolf & Goats	*44*
22	Serpent & Rich Man	*46*
23	Lion & Fox	*48*
24	Frogs, Oak, Serpent	*51*

25	Sheep, Ram, Lion	54
26	Ass, Bees, Wasp	55
27	A Planted Tree & Reeds	57
28	Mouse, Sun, Cloud, Wind, Wall	58
29	Crow & Other Birds	60
30	Ox, Lion, Ram	62
31	Young Dog & Old Dog	62
32	Cock & Hen	63
33	Brazen Pot & Clay Pot	65
34	Frog & Oxen	66
35	Mouse & Hole	67
36	Wolf & Cattle	69
37	Eagle, Fowl, Lion, Beasts, Bat	71
38	Hare & Hounds	73
39	Starling, Eagle, Birds	75
40	Bear & Doe	76
41	Peacock, Wheat, Crane	78
42	Smith & Bramblebush	79
43	Wolf, Dog, Flock	80
44	Kite & Doves	82
45	Cormorant & Birds	83
46	Cat & Mouse	85
47	Ass in Lion's Skin	87
48	Fox & Crane	89
49	Sow, Doe, Beasts	91
50	Lion, Beasts, Ape	93
51	Four Oxen & a Lion	94
52	Lion, Wolf, Fox, Ox, Calf	95
53	Sun, Wind, Man	97
54	Cedar & Bush	99
55	Small Fish in Net	100
56	Lion & Hunter	101
57	He-Goat & Lion	103

58 Boy & Man   104
59 Lion & Toad   106
60 Bullock & Ox   107
61 Lion & Dog   108
62 Wolves, Goats, Dog   110
63 Cock & Hen   112
64 A Bird Buildeth Her Nest in the Grain   113
65 Lion & Ass   115
66 Mule & Fox   117
67 Two Apes & a Lion   118
68 Lion, Man, Pit, Snake   120
69 Wolf, Fox, Dove   124
70 Lion & Cattle   126
71 Starling & Princess   128
72 Ram & Ten Ewes   131
73 Flea & Camel   133
74 Stag & Dogs   134
75 Wolf & Shepherd   136
76 Sun & Moon   138
77 Viper & Man   139
78 Ape & King   141
79 Ape & Fox   144
80 Woman, Husband, Knight, Vizier   145
81 A Sick Man, His Daughter, a Physician   147
82 Ewe, Goat, Shepherd   149
83 Thief & Witch   150
84 Horse, Merchant, Man   152
85 Lion, Wolf, Bear, Fox   154
86 Hen & Mistress   156
87 Camel & Caravan   158
88 Osprey & Pot   160
89 A Fearsome & Awesome Knight   161
90 Fly & Ox   164

91	Wolf & Fox	165
92	A Goring Ox & His Master	166
93	The Man of the Field Knoweth Hunting	167
94	Fox & Cat	169
95	Image & Man	171
96	Conies & Hare	173
97	Lion, Goats, Fox	175
98	Raven & Carcass	177
99	Fox, Wagon, Fish	178
100	Demon & Ship	182
101	Merchant, Robbers, Knight	183
102	Camel & Mountain Goat	186
103	A Man Ploughing His Tilth	188
104	The Ape, His Two Sons, a Leopard	190
105	Boar, Lion, Fox	191
106	The Lion & His Son	193
107	Elephant & Hunter	201
108	Cat, Bird, Fox, Hare	204
109	Crab, Frogs, Crane	205
110	Ant & Mouse	207
111	Spider, King, Slave	209
112	Man, Rock, Mouse	212
113	Man & Wolf	213
114	Chameleon & Merchants	215
115	An Old Man & His Sons, a Captain & His Men	217
116	An Old Man, His Son, a Fish, the Leviathan	218
117	Wolf & Fox	220
118	Youth, Rogues, Woman, Judge	222
119	The Envious Man & The Covetous	227

Preface

IT IS not surprising that Moses Hadas should have undertaken to translate *Fables of a Jewish Aesop*. Combining Jewish and Greek thought and literature was a central concern in his life. Moses, my father, was a Jewish classicist who taught in the Department of Greek and Latin at Columbia University. He grew up in Atlanta, and many people thought of him as very Southern. When he wanted to be, Moses could also be very Jewish. He used to tell a story about being able to join in the chanting of psalms in a Greek synagogue after World War II. He loved to sing, and he could figure out the notes assigned to each of the musical marks in the Massoretic text. He was proud, too, of telling off an Orthodox rabbi on a ship sailing from Palestine. The rabbi had been eating unkosher food and talking to women in ways that Moses knew were against Orthodox Jewish law, and Moses quoted to him the relevant passages from the *Shulhan Arukh*, the authoritative sixteenth-century Jewish code of law. The rabbi, Moses reported, behaved properly thereafter. Moses was proud, too, of being told he spoke Yiddish "as if he had just gotten off the boat" from Poland. In fact he had gotten off the boat when he was too young to speak any language fluently.

Despite his ability to be deeply Jewish, Moses spent the majority of his time with his Greek interests. He loved Greek literature and taught it until months before he died. Plutarch and not the Talmud contained the values he tried to live by. But it was the fusion between the Greeks and others that was the center of his scholarly interests. His best and most important book was *Hellenistic Culture: Fusion and Diffusion* (Columbia University Press, 1959). Like many Jews who lived before Hitler gave anti-Semitism a bad name, he desperately wanted the fusion to work. He wanted to be accepted as a teacher of the classics even though he was Jewish. That was not easy at Columbia, where he was one of the first Jews on the faculty. According to William M. Calder III, the treatment of Moses was "the second most blatant example of anti-Semitism in American classics." Calder reports that Moses was not "made a member of the faculty until 1952," when he was fifty-two years old.[1]

Translating *Fables of a Jewish Aesop* was a way, then, for Moses Hadas to show that Jews belonged to the humanistic tradition. One couldn't make this point simply by pointing to the Bible. Many people didn't consider the Old Testament Jewish; it wasn't yet customary to refer to "the Hebrew Bible." To show that Jews after Jesus could contribute not only to science but to the humanities was a constant struggle. The fact that Jews could participate in the tradition of fable writing was a small thing but not a trivial one. That Berechiah wrote in rhymed prose, a form not used in the Hebrew Bible, showed in a small way that Hebrew was a live language in which new things could be done. It is possible to see this translation as an assertion by Moses that he, like Berechiah, was part of the western world and had a little something to say.

According to the moral of Fable 52, "A man must not hasten to speak before one that is stronger than he." This comes at the end of a fable in which a fox is discreet when he talks to a lion; he has just seen the

<hr>

[1] William M. Calder III, *Men in Their Books: Studies in the Modern History of Classical Scholarship*, edited by John F. Harris and R. Scott Smith, p. 267, n. 27. *Spudasmata*, Band 67. George Olms Verlag.

wolf killed for giving the lion advice he didn't like. Moses had to be a little like the fox — to speak but to be careful about what he said. He had gone to school in Atlanta with a grandson of Joel Chandler Harris, the collector of many fables including the one about Br'er Rabbit, who, like the fox in Berechiah, had to learn how to speak carefully in a world filled with people ready to snap your head off.

DAVID HADAS
St. Louis, Missouri
May 1999

Introduction

Fables in the Western European Tradition

ALTHOUGH the exact dates of the life of the author of the *Fox Fables*, Berechiah ben Natronai ha-Nakdan, are much disputed, it can be stated with certainty that the fables were written at the end of the twelfth century or the beginning of the thirteenth and that the author must therefore have been dependent on the collections of fables then available in western Europe. The Greek texts of Aesop were available in Constantinople, but there is no evidence of their being known in the West at that time. There the Aesopic tradition was represented by a number of Latin fable collections. The best-known of these was the so-called *Romulus* collection, of which several manuscripts are extant. The earliest dates from the tenth century. The number of fables in this collection differs according to the manuscript: The manuscript in Corpus Christi College, Oxford, has forty-five fables; that of Munich, thirty-nine; that of Bern, forty-seven. The total from all sources is eighty. The order of the fables is closely related, although by no means identical, in all the manuscripts.

The chief source of the *Romulus* collection was the work of the Roman poet Phaedrus (fl. c. A.D. 14–60). Some thirty-seven of the *Romulus* fables are derived from his poems, and it is generally believed that most of the others are adapted from fables of his which are no longer extant. It is hardly necessary to add that the *Romulus* collection does not contain all the fables which appear in the Greek collections attributed to Aesop. The different *Romulus* manuscripts have various prefaces in which the origin of the selection of fables is "explained." The commonest explanation is that an emperor named Romulus chose them for his son, sometimes called Tiberius. It is impossible to make even an informed guess about the true origin of the collection.

The fables in the *Romulus* collection are in prose—often no more than prose adaptations of the verse fables of Phaedrus. There is, however, another collection of fables which is clearly based on the prose *Romulus* but is written in elegiac verse. It is often referred to as the *Anonymus Neveleti*, because it was published, without an author's name, by Nevelet in Frankfurt in 1610. Many scholars now accept its attribution (proposed by Hervieux) to Galterus Anglicus, who wrote about 1177. There are sixty fables in the collection, all of which can be found in the prose *Romulus*. The collection was very popular, and numerous translations and adaptations were made into the vernacular languages.

Although there is no lack of such fable material which can be dated before the thirteenth century, it is highly probable that there was a great deal more which has since been lost. The story (Fable 85 in this collection) of the sick lion who was cured by being wrapped, on the advice of the fox, in the skin torn from a wolf, is to be found in the Greek Aesop but not in any of the early medieval Latin fable collections. Yet there is an adaptation of it in a poem by Paulus Diaconus in the early ninth century, and it appears at greater length in the *Ecbasis captivi* (*Escape of a Certain Captive*), probably written about 940, and in numerous beast epics of the twelfth century. Whether it appeared in a fable collection now lost or was transmitted orally can no longer be determined.

The tradition of Aesop was also represented in the Middle Ages by the fables of Avianus, an author whose dates are very uncertain—conjectures vary between the second and the sixth centuries A.D. These fables were to a large degree different from those in the *Romulus* collection and they also were adapted into both prose and verse by such authors as Alexander Neckham, in his *Novus Avianus*, and the "Astensis poeta" (c.1100).

There was one other source of medieval fable material, which had no direct connection with Aesop, the *Panchatantra*. This consists of Indian fables which entered Persia in the sixth century, some of which were incorporated into the *Kalila and Dimna*, originally written in Persian, and translated into Arabic in the eighth century. The work was essentially a frame story into which various animal fables were fitted. The form remained constant in the numerous adaptations into other languages, of which the most important for western Europe was the *Novus Aesopus* of Baldo (c.1190). This work, probably based on a Latin prose version of *Kalila and Dimna*, consisted of 1242 leonine hexameters and contained thirty-five fables. Twenty of these are the same as those found in another adaptation of *Kalila and Dimna*, the *Directorium humanae vitae* of John of Capua, but it is unlikely that there was any direct influence. Few of Baldo's fables have any direct counterparts in the *Romulus* collections or the Hebrew *Fox Fables* but it is possible that his work was known to Berechiah.

We have named only a few of the extant fable collections of the Middle Ages. Since there were undoubtedly many more which have not survived, it is pointless to try to discover the precise source of each of the Hebrew fox tales. One possible connection, however, should be described in a little more detail: the fables of Marie de France. These are very close in time to the fables of Berechiah, since they were written in the latter part of the twelfth century, probably between 1170 and 1180. All scholars agree that Marie used a source written in English, but that it was not the fable collection of King Alfred mentioned in her prologue. There are in her work a large number of fables from the standard *Romulus* collections; a few demonstrably from Eastern sources; some from the beast epic *Roman de Renart*, which was rapidly becoming popular in the twelfth century; and a few about human beings, which may have derived from contemporary anecdotes or orally transmitted tales. There remain, however, a number of fables from sources completely unknown, and it is thus the more remarkable that many of these appear not only in Marie's collection but also in the *Fox Fables* of Berechiah. Of the thirteen such fables found in both authors, seven have precisely the same plot, and six show a basic resemblance. Another thirty-seven of the Hebrew *Fox Fables* are to be found both in Marie's work and in the standard *Romulus* collections, and it is clear from correspondences of detail that Berechiah was using the work of Marie rather than the Latin versions. This does not mean that the Latin collections were unknown to him. Fable 48 in Berechiah's work, for example, is found in *Romulus* but not in Marie's collection, and there are others in which the *Romulus* versions obviously have been used. Twenty-seven of Berechiah's fables seem to have been taken from those of Avianus, and others from the *Kalila and Dimna*. For twenty-seven of his fables, no source can be found.

The uncertainties about the exact dates of both Marie de France and Berechiah preclude any final decision about which of them was the source for the other, but all the evidence we have indicates that Berechiah drew on the collection of Marie de France. It is very likely that she wrote her collection while he was still very young, or perhaps even before his birth. There is also internal evidence that he used her work. Fable 41 of Marie's collection tells of two *serfs* who did not wish to discuss something in their master's hearing. In several manuscripts the critical word was transcribed as *cerfs* [stags], and it was a manuscript containing this error that Berechiah used for his fable of the two deer (Fable 19). The story surely has more point when the speakers are serfs. We may therefore say that Berechiah almost certainly used the collection of Marie de France as his main source.

xvi

He did not observe the order in which her fables are collected, however, and to the fables he derived from her work he added numerous others from the main sources of fables available to him, chiefly the *Romulus* and Avianus collections. The few fables he derived from Arabic sources are very probably taken from Latin adaptations of *Kalila and Dimna*. Although it is possible that he invented some or all of those stories for which no source is known, it is much more probable that they were based upon sources now lost or on Hebrew oral tradition.

The Author

THERE is very little definite information about the life of Rabbi Berechiah ben Natronai ha-Nakdan. It is known, however, that he was French, born perhaps in Burgundy, and that he spent much time in Provence. There is also evidence that he was the same person as the Benedictus le Puncteur mentioned in an Oxford document of the late twelfth century, for Berechiah means "blessed" (*benedictus*) and ha-Nakdan means "the punctuator" (*le puncteur*). It must be admitted, however, that the term was frequently applied to Jewish scribes and grammarians; so the identification is not completely certain.

There is considerable disagreement among scholars about the exact dates of Berechiah's life. The consensus is that he wrote his works at the end of the twelfth century, but some critics would place them rather in the first half of the thirteenth. The point is of some significance, since so many fable collections and beast epics were appearing at the time that a difference of even ten or twenty years could markedly affect the number of possible sources. Fortunately, there can be no chronological objection to assuming that he knew the work of Marie de France. And if he was in England, as the Oxford document may indicate, it would be even more likely that he had firsthand knowledge of the work of Marie de France, which was written there toward the end of the twelfth century. The *Fox Fables* (*Mishle Shualim*) are Berechiah's best-known work, but he produced several others, among them a lapidary, *Koah ha-Abanim* [the power of stones], and an imitation of the *Natural Questions* of Adelhard of Bath, *Dodi we Nechdi* [uncle and nephew].

The Work

BY NO means all the "fox fables" of Berechiah are about the relation of the fox with other animals. The title can probably be explained by the contemporary popularity of the *Roman de Renart*—the involved account, appearing in many branches, of the struggle between the cunning and unscrupulous fox Renart and the greedy and stupid wolf Isengrim. Several of Berechiah's fables are in fact taken from some version of the *Roman de Renart*. We have mentioned that the sources of many of the *Fox Fables* are known, but this does not mean that Berechiah merely translated or adapted them. Not only are details frequently changed, but sometimes even the kinds of animals taking part are different, either because the author felt that those substituted were more suitable for his setting, or because there was no word for the animals in his source, in the Old Testament Hebrew which he used. The fables are in rhymed prose, with a large amount of Biblical references and quotation. Indeed, it may be said that some of the stories are centos of Old Testament quotation. The didactic element is stressed, as it always is in fables, and it may well be that here, as so often in the beast epic, there are numerous references to contemporary personages and events which we can no longer identify but which would have amused the relatively restricted audience for which the fables were intended. Berechiah's purpose was social and moral instruction, combined perhaps with gentle satire. The language he used was inevitably that of the Old

Testament but there is no evidence in his work of any stress on religion.

The Translation

THE translation is based on the critical text of the original edited by A. M. Haberman, *Mishle Shualim l'Rabbi Bere-khyah ha-Naqdan* (Jerusalem, Schocken Publishing House, Ltd., 1945–1946). No attempt has been made to reproduce the rhymed prose of the original, but the translator has taken great care to indicate the very numerous Old Testament reminiscences and quotations by incorporating the wording of the corresponding passages of the King James Version of the Bible. The result is a translation which not only reflects the style of the original but which also has a Biblical flavor highly appropriate to the gentle and at times ironic advice which the fables convey. Thus readers of the English translation can be aware of what is perhaps the most interesting feature of Berechiah's work —the change which Aesop's fables underwent when viewed in the mirror of medieval Hebrew culture.

While this book was in press, the news came of the death of Moses Hadas. This is thus the last work of a man who contributed as much as anyone to the understanding and perpetuation of the humanistic tradition. It is perhaps fitting that this work, whose translation gave him great pleasure in the making, reflects that union of the Hebrew, Greek, and Latin traditions of which he himself was so fine a representative.

W. T. H. JACKSON

Fables of a Jewish Aesop

Author's Proem

SAITH Rabbi Berechiah ben Natronai ha-Nakdan:
To impart prudence to the simple, to the young
knowledge and astuteness, my heart inditeth goodly matter, wherewith to satisfy hearts like a garden well-watered,
with parables of foxes and beasts. Verily these parables are
current upon the lips of all earth's progeny, and men of
diverse tongues have set them forth in a book. But my
practices are different from their practices, for I have enlarged and augmented them with like and similar matter,
in verses and poems, like sapphires veiled. Whoso reads
them will attain many things choicer than fine gold and
precious rubies, as the eyes of them that look forthright
will perceive.

Blessed be our Rock, who hath given man mouth to
speak, and hand to write words and compose them, and
eye to behold them that ascend and them that descend,
and ear to hear instruction.

The saying of Berechiah ben Natronai ha-Nakdan, who
caused these parables to sprout and gave them birth:
How could I look on at their perishing? If I wrote them
not down for a memorial, what profit in my labor? If I be
accounted a fool or hasty, yet is my tongue the pen of a
ready scribe. Would that my words be inscribed! The
fortune of the pen which writeth my parables is upon the
world's revolving wheel, which is obscure to the eyes of
my understanding—a vagabond upon an island of the sea
am I. These it slayeth and these it letteth live. It spreadeth
abroad over the wide places of the earth to wreak breach

upon breach, and with its chariot wheel confounds the righteous until they are consumed. By its devices the course of its chariot is perverse; it charges upon the good and humbles them, upon the evil and delivers them. When it sees Truth standing in the plain and laying her hand to the spindle, it smites her in the fifth rib and lifts the sickle against her feet and hews them off and crushes them, the flesh along with the bone. It degrades her from being mistress, as though she had conceived in harlotry and had become blemished and walked bowed down. Instead it loves Falsehood, and to him extends the golden scepter, and summons him to its presence, and he finds grace and favor in its eyes; it sets him up upon his feet and adorns him with comely shoes and brings all his friends and kinsmen near and keeps his enemies and them that scorn him afar, until the workers of iniquity have ascended as on stairs. They have framed slanders to cut off sucklings and sprigs and twigs from the poor and needy and all who do not as they do. Weapons of war are in their mouths: Their lips are swords, their teeth spears and darts, to reduce the humble to be trampled like the mire of the streets. Few, therefore, are they who mend the breaches, for the wicked are supported while the knowing ones are without favor. The righteous groan, but the bitter are sweet; the sons of evil ascend but the lofty are abased. Prayer is folly, praise slander, sacrifice iniquity, prudence scorn. Their root is open to falsehood; they walk forth with a high hand; by their own name they call upon lands, which are thus likened to cattle. But men of righteousness are like a hedge of thorns, like untempered mortar. They that dwell upon the heights, the lofty among men, are abased in darkness and thick mist; their heads are bowed down like a reed, and they are fearful of the voice of the multitude, men whom their fathers despised. They abide in their towns and castles; they are compassed about with pride and haughtiness as with a chain. They covet silver and love gold, but are reluctant to put their hands forth to their wealth. They lie with their tongues, and yield not their necks to the service of their Creator. They titivate themselves with pride, but bestow no gifts. They are waxed fat and shine; in all their craft and guile, in spoliation and overreaching, in smooth flattery, they succeed and prosper, even as the days that they encamp. But he that walketh in righteousness and speaketh uprightly is in thick and disordered darkness. From the noise of the scornful archers my twigs have burgeoned and I make bold to direct my pen to a parable against falsehood, which holds sway, enthroned above the exalted ones of the city, whereas truth is bereft, and he that turns aside from evil is confounded, and the wicked gloats over his desire, and the face of the world is filled with vain folk who wreak abomination. They that honor God are lightly esteemed, but their pursuers are fleet of foot. Alas! Truth, which stood fast, hath been snared in a gin, and the vile have mounted upward while the gentle have descended to the pit. Every head has been rendered a tail, and every rogue and thief has attained dominion. The ways of truth are curtailed and hidden, but deception is augmented and conspicuous. In the eyes of the rich the poor are like bears, but they that love the rich are many. The foolish take root, but the wise is sated with penury. They multiply and grow strong, they wink their eyes and make them hard. Brotherly kisses are hooks in their jaws; they that hope for sweet counsel of fellowship will find them evil, slanderers in secret. He will say, "Eat thy fill"; with his lips he praises but inwardly he curses. He bows down and kneels, but his thoughts are only to work injury.

The wheel which weldeth these diversities passes over us incessantly. Wrathfully it smites and afflicts all whose palate studies truth; but whoso boasts himself of a false gift, his honor is measureless, though it be clouds and wind without rain. The vile and nameless, with burning lips and a wicked heart, will lengthen his days and see seed. He is clothed in a robe of fine linen and swathed with an ample garment about his neck. But peace hath nought, it hath no garment. All they that deal treacherously are very happy. With flattering lips he destroys his neighbor; he embraces and kisses him, and he flatters him with his mouth, but in his heart lurks iniquity, his ambush is within him. He is drenched in wickedness, and he supplants every brother by the heel. When I behold such a conjuncture as this I curse.

And I plied my poesy and said:

Lament, my pen, over the chariot wheel,
Which revolves and rolls, overturns and destroys.
Fallen is the tongue of truth, falsehood is risen high.
Pure prayer is folly; the innocent head is covered with
    shame.
Praise is slander; wickedness is exalted.
The right hand of wrong is in the ascendant;
The guiltless, vanished and scorned.
In the island of the sea is a congregation bereft of wit,
A base breed, crowned with shame.
The ear of its many rich is uncircumcised
For them that ask, but for them that give, circumcised.
The treacherous frame false charges
To plunder the upright of cloak and tunic.
The congregation of flatterers rejoices and is jubilant,
But in the camp of the upright wailing is heard.
They bless lips that utter abomination,
And curse the speakers of verity.
Evil is like good, hag like virgin,
Like sweet, bitter, light like darkness.
Berechiah curses and abjures the times
And their fortunes, small or great.
Better a dry crust with toil, apart from them,
Than to share a heritage with them.

When I reflected upon this, my thoughts confounded me and sleep fled from my eyes that I might commit to secret discourse the words with which I am filled. I say to him under whose eye my writing shall come, "Eat this scroll, for out of the eater shall come forth meat, and sense shall issue from the sensible." Let him who reflects on my parables not say, "As a thorn goeth up into the hand of a drunkard, so is a parable in the mouth of fools," a mass of dreams and vanity; for only from the wicked does wickedness come forth, but from deliverers, deliverance. And if a man make his palate rebel against me—"the wisdom of the prudent is to understand his way."

Lo, I draw parables of beasts and birds to strengthen hands that are weak, and of creeping things that crawl upon the ground; these are for a similitude for them that walk on earth. I shall begin with the lion who rules over them all, great and small, for they changed his honor for shame. So when a rich man grows poor, his comrades make themselves strangers to him.

I

Lion, Beasts, Cattle

MANY ARE THE LOVERS OF THE RICH
MAN WHEN HIS SPLENDOR SHINES;
BUT WHEN HE IS HUMBLED AND HIS
POWER CURTAILED, THEY CHANGE.

ONCE there was a lion, old and sick, whose loins were
diseased, so that his spirit panted in travail; his fate
was uncertain, whether he would live or die. To behold
the lion's discomfiture there came all cattle and beasts,
even from the desolate ends of the earth: some for love to
visit the sick, some to see his anguish, some to succeed to
his rule, some to know who would reign after him. So
grievous was his malady that none could discern whether
he were yet alive or already dead. The ox came and gored
him, to try whether his strength were ended and empty;

7

the heifer trampled him with her hoofs; the fox nipped
the lappets of his ears with his teeth; the ewe brushed his
moustaches with her tail, and said: "When will he die and
his name perish?" And the cock pecked at his eyes, and
broke his teeth with gravel. Then the lion's spirit returned, and he perceived that his enemies were gloating
over him, and he lamented: "Alas for the day when my
trusted counselors despise me, when my power and glory
have turned to my bane, when my erstwhile slaves lord it
over me and they who loved me aforetime are become
my enemies."

The parable is of a man filled with riches and honor
whose neighbors serve him all. But when the day of
calamity comes upon him, when he is bowed down and
his power humbled, then they stand afar from his plague
and separate from him and strip him of his righteousness,
and despise him they had chosen.

And I, Berechiah, when I beheld this rebelliousness
frowardly visited upon a noble, I plied my poesy and said
in my song:

Woe to the lions prostrate before a calf,
To the chieftains who kiss a foot!
The feet of the faithful are trodden in mire,
And the sons of falsehood have raised their banner
   high.
Debased are the rulers, and the wicked exalted.
The unrighteous exult;
Truth is reduced to slavery,
A queen become a handmaiden.
Now hath truth no feet;
Falsehood's flattering tongue hath ravished them.

2

Mouse, Frog, Eagle

HE THAT DIGGETH A PIT WILL BE
REQUITED ACCORDING TO THE
FRUIT OF HIS DEEDS.

A MOUSE sat at the threshold of the gristmill, his lips
and jowls covered with meal. As the sun shone upon
him and upon the palms of his hands and feet, he luxuri-
ated and fondled his whiskers, as was the manner of his
father and all his folk. And as he abode there without fear
or qualm a frog happened to pass and paused to investigate the state of the mouse: "Is the master of the house
present?" Answered the mouse: "Mine is the house and
mine the grain, and mine the seed in the granary, whether
for food or trade. This is my house and refuge, and I fill
my hole with provision. When the upper and nether
millstones are at rest, I too rest at their side, and they provide me abundant food, for both are filled with flour.
Such is my wont all my days. And when I hear a multitude of folk I hide in my crannies, and emerge again when
no man is nigh, and gather my provisions." The frog observed that all the mouse's members, his hands and the
smooth of his neck were white, and she said: "Why is
your habit hoar; has age sprinkled your hair?" And he replied: "With whiteness is my dwelling, and of fine
wheaten flour have I tasted, and the meal has flowed over
me and spread broadcast, for the doors of meal and of
flour are not shut in my face." Then said the frog in her
cunning: "All your life is fear and trembling. Why do
you glory in fine flour and dainties, when your life hangs
suspended before you? All that approach your lodging

confound and affright you; every gathering of people, every sound, terrifies you, for all seek to entrap you. Your food is hard and dry, your clothing always dusty. But my dress is clean and shiny, and in my abode no enemy lurks; and my food is fat and sweet. You are beset with snares, but my dwelling place is secure. Hearken to my words and my discourse: I shall supply all your wants. Come willingly with me to my shelter of reeds and clay." The frog overwhelmed him with the smoothness of her lips, and strutted before him and flexed her thighs. The mouse took no heed until they came to the river's bank, when he said to the frog: "Where is the house where you dwell?" She answered: "Across the river. There you will see all that is in my tent, the good things your heart desires. Turn your face to the river and cross its calm waters, spreading your limbs as if to do obeisance." But the mouse was apprehensive for his life and hesitated to go forward, for he had never made trial of water. And he said: "Where is the abode you spoke of? Who will cross the sea for us? In traversing waters I am untried; better for me to sojourn at home and there abide all the days of my life, for the way before me is perverse." Said the frog: "Hear me, good sir. In your crossing the water I shall be with you, and the streams shall not drown you. The enemies who pursue you, you shall leave far behind. This cord bind to my foot and yours. Your feet shall stand on the surface; and I shall go with you to guide your path, by this thread which you tie to my thigh, by deed and by word. No harm shall befall you; you shall flourish amidst brethren. Now shall you see whether my words come to pass." Said the mouse: "If it is as you say I shall make a covenant with you. Show your thigh and cross the river." The frog's eloquence deceived him, and they compacted together. Frog and mouse proceeded apace, joined by the cord attached to their legs. When they reached the depths of the abyss the frog thought to submerge the mouse and bring him down to the pit. And as the mouse mustered his strength on the surface of the water an eagle traversing the sky noticed that the two were entangled with one another, and flew to the prey. Fierce was the eagle, and pitiless. He spread his pinions and seized them; they were ensnared by the strong cord which bound them together, and could not separate. The eagle was ravenous, but when he saw he could not reach the mouse because of the thick hide drawn tight over his back and the black hairs that sprouted from it, he turned his attention to the frog, which he found goodly to behold and pleasant to eat, and swallowed her down at a single gulp. The mouse turned this way and that, and when he perceived that his fetters were broken, he set his feet for rapid flight, and escaped, himself alone. The frog, which was fastened at his side, fell into the snare she herself had spread; her deed was returned upon her head.

This parable I apply to a man who digs a foul pit to ensnare his neighbor—who flatters him to mislead him. But his guile is his own punishment; his deeds return upon his own head, all that he devised against his neighbor. The innocent escapes to his tent unharmed. And so hath Solomon said in his wisdom [Proverbs 11.19]: "He that pursueth evil pursueth it to his own death."

I plied my poesy and said:

Folly was the cunning the frog devised.
Freed was the mouse, and safe returned
To his granary filled with grain. Neither devoured
Nor buried was he, nor imprisoned, nor crushed.
She that spake honeyed words perished, nor returned
To her forest home. Such is the requital
For the beguilement of smooth lips; of no avail,
The deceptions of the false heart; ill devised,
For the neighbor finds the deviser and destroys him.
But the righteous shall dwell in the land,
And they that seek goodness and cherish purity.

3

Wolf & Sheep at the River

EACH TURNETH TO HIS OWN PROFIT,
AND IF HE BE POOR HE WILL OPPRESS
HIS BROTHER.

A WOLF walked solitary to the river to quench his thirst, and there espied a sheep standing opposite him at a distance. The wolf called out: "Wherefore hast thou troubled me? Mine is this river, I made it." The sheep replied in innocence, with words goodly and sweet: "My lord king, I have not troubled you. Master over my head have I held you all my days. I went forth from my tent to drink the river's waters; if this displeases you I shall return. Your words brook no challenge." The wolf spoke harshly to the sheep, saying: "Who are you not to dread me? Do wolf and sheep feed together? Has anyone beheld them together quenching their thirst at water courses? You have troubled my water and I cannot drink, but must return thirsty because of my shame. Your primal ancestor sinned against me in word and deed; for four years he rebelled and transgressed." The sheep replied: "Wherefore doth my lord so cruelly mock me? I am only a little sheep, not yet a year old. Why do you devise quarrels against your neighbor? Sons should not die for their fathers' failings." Answered the wolf: "It is because of you that I am thirsty and dishonored therefore shall you never more behold me." Thereupon he smote the sheep and stripped his fleece and tore his flesh and devoured him.

The parable applies to everyone who pursues his own profit. He that is stronger than his neighbor swallows him down. So do the judges and the bailiffs who pervert the justice of men and ransack their purses for silver and strip them of their fine garments in their very presence. The sage's saying is current [Proverbs 13.23]: "For want of judgment is a man destroyed."

And I plied my poesy and said:

Fools love folly, scorners scorn;
Harshly speaks the rich man to him whose words
    are complaisant.

4

Cock & Gem

THE FOOL DEPRIVE   HIS EYES
OF WISDOM; HE DESPISES GOOD
AND CHOOSES EVIL.

A COCK mounted a midden heap and with his claws scattered and uncovered the dung to find worms for his food, as it was his habit to search for food there. He found the gem called jasper, and would scratch in the midden no more. Said he: "I thought to find some profit in my toil, some worm or fly to nourish me. But it is you that I see, jasper, and of what advantage is my finding you? True, you are handsome to look at, and if some rich man found you he would be proud. He would grasp you in his hand, set you in fine gold, and your glow would be multiplied sevenfold. But now you are trampled and trodden underfoot; my soul has no pity upon you, for you do not satisfy my desire. Better for me a worm, or even half of one, to restore my famished soul, than the finding of a precious stone."

This parable I find abundantly applicable to a man who scorns the honorable and withholds his eye from the righteous, who spurns the good and prefers the evil. Such is his rule and statute, but it touches him not until the hour of his need. And so said Solomon in his proverb [Proverbs 13.13]: "Whoso despiseth a thing shall be constricted by it."

Against him I raised my voice to revile him in my poesy:

The man whose heart turns from desiring wise counsel
Is like the cock who forsakes the jasper in muck and
    mire.
In his heart sprouts an ulcer; the loathsome
Is his desire, the honorable he esteems lightly
As a thing scorned and despised. Contemptuousness
He likens to discernment; filth, to cleanliness,
To choice gems set in gold.

5

Dog, Cheese, Water

WHAT DOES NOT SUPPLY A NEED
GIVES NO PLEASURE; EYES ARE NOT
SATISFIED WITH MERELY LOOKING.

A DOG seized a cheese in the house and carried it hi ther and yon in his mouth and turned this way and that, until his path took him to a bridge, from which he loo ke d down into the water. When he saw the reflection of the cheese held in his teeth he said to himself: "If I had the cheese in the water together with that in my mouth, the two would be better than one." His plan was to incline his head like a reed and so swallow the gobbet in the water. But when he opened his mouth and parted his teeth to grasp what was not his, the morsel he had seized in the beginning fell from his mouth, and he found himself plucked on this side and on that. He emerged from the water with nothing to show for all his effort.

I have observed this trait in the man whose heart is full of desire. Though he is laden with silver and gold, he covets all—and loses all. I am pleased with Solomon's proverb [Proverbs 13.7]: "Be thou content with what thou hast in thy hand and thy possession; and envy not that which is another's."

And I plied my poesy and said:

Heaven vouchsafed sustenance to all living creatures,
But oft they covet twice their need.
He that covets and ravins more than his portion
Will fare as did the dog with the cheese in the water;
He thought to add to what was enough,
And lost provision for two days.

6

Fox & Fishes

MANY GIVE COUNSEL IN THEIR
OWN BEHOOF, TO DRAW OTHERS
UP BY THEIR HOOK.

A FOX walking by a river bank saw one fish hastening to escape while another fish pursued him. Overtaking him, the second fish attacked him with animosity, and the two fought, with none to deliver between them, each charging angrily against the other. The fox said not a word, but approached the water in the hope that he could sink his teeth into them or trap them by the snare of his cunning. But the waters proved a barrier to his lust, so he turned thence to another spot, where he addressed them with no hesitation. When he saw the fish fighting, the great oppressing the small, the gentry snapping at the lowly, and the war between them growing heated, he called out to them: "Are all of you such fools that quiet is impossible? Is this the covenant among you and the sole statute of your congregation: that each destroy his neighbor, that the larger swallow his companion which is smaller and hew him asunder on the slightest provocation? If all the fish of the sea would assemble and say to me 'Rule over us,' I would not forsake my resolve, for all the day they are in terror and confusion; each fights his brother, every man his neighbor. Perverse is the path before them with their bowstrings drawn and weapons whetted, and on this path they wander astray, knowing naught of the path of peace. Hear now the logic of my discourse; incline your ears and come unto me. Depart from thence and come hither. In joy shall you go forth and in peace, if you hearken to my counsel, and ye shall bless me also. Depart from the sea to dry land, and together we shall inherit the earth. Then shall your tranquillity be increased, and nation shall not lift sword against nation, for none shall cause a breach. Serene and untroubled shall all the world abide, and the joy of wild asses shall be ours. Hearts that are troubled shall be refreshed, and all the inhabitants of earth shall shout for gladness upon their couches of ease, by day and by night without surcease. None shall do evil, none destroy." But one of the fish replied: "If thou wilt verily rule over us, wilt thou indeed ordain peace for us? Even when we abide in quiet waters, surrounded by our kin and in peace, the robber assails us, the destroyer rises against us, and we live in terror of men's snares. Many fishermen fish for us, many hunters hunt us; we all roar like bears. If you had experience of our plight, your anguish would equal ours. If now by thy cunning thou devourest spoil, when thou hast done spoiling thou shalt thyself be spoiled, for suddenly thy creditors shall rise up against thee and thy ways will not prosper. How dost thou spread a web of deceit against us and count thyself secure in a land of peace? Surely the fowl of the heavens and the fish of the sea and the beasts of the field all are ambushed and hunted, and even humans quarrel for the envy that is between them. But there be higher than they, and he that is higher than the highest regardeth."

This proverb counsels vigilance against those who advise for their own advantage. Beware of their seduction, for by earth's transgression flatterers have multiplied, and the face of this generation is as the face of a dog. Every man must be aware of him that would destroy; but the wise man hath his eyes in his head.

And I plied my poesy:

The face of this generation is the face of a dog;

They speak with two hearts.
Their words are like butter, their thoughts tallow.
They press the breasts for pleasure,
As a nursling drawing milk.
Spies are they, but there is no Joshua nor Caleb among
them.

7

Dog, Sheep, Lion, Wolf, Bear

INFINITE IS THE EVIL WHEN A
RULER GIVES EAR TO FALSEHOOD.

A DOG cried loudly against a sheep before the lion and
his assessors, saying: "My lord, have mercy on thy
servant. Yesterday this sheep stole from me a loaf of
bread which I had laid up for my provision." The sheep
answered: "This is not true; if aught of it be found with
your servant, it shall be death." Said the judge to the dog:
"Have you witnesses to corroborate your tale?" The dog
replied: "Aye, my words are right and true, and I call
upon credible witnesses to testify. The wolf and the eagle
saw this sheep in my house, which she had entered without my permission, and she carried the bread out between
her legs. Take no pity upon her." The witnesses were instructed to render their testimony on an appointed day,
which suited their honor and dignity, and they took
counsel together to make their accounts match. One falsehood they fitted to its fellow to make their lies uniform.
The day came and they entered the court; the judges, who
had been bribed, examined the case and studied it, but
came to a single conclusion. Even the judges corroborated

the dog's charge and supported him. The ear is accustomed to falsehood, and man transgresses for a crust of bread; therefore was the judgment perverted. They enjoined the sheep to pay according to the weight of the bread which she had purloined. She returned sighing and groaning, for she had nothing at home. So she sold her fleece, and the shearers foregathered. Before her shearers the sheep was mute. With the fleece shorn from her back she bought bread, and she returned that which she had not ravished. But her anguish was sore, for the heat afflicted her and the sun dealt obdurately with her. And when the chill of winter came her flesh was harried with cold, for there was no fleece to protect her skin. She would not be comforted for the sake of the bread, and her sorrows for her little ones increased; Rachel [sheep] was weeping for her children. Winter came on and snow reached to the knees, and there Rachel died by the way. For this the wolf and the eagle had waited, and upon the news of the sheep they came to the field where her body had been cast, and said: "For our reward and for our testimony this flesh shall come between our teeth; let each serve his soul with this flesh before it be cut off."

The parable is for a generation whose teeth are as swords when they conspire to devour the meek. Each hardens his face. Not to have committed violence or deceit is for them an abomination. Each seeks his own blemish in his fellow; and the ruler hearkens to falsehood. The one slanders, and the other presses the charge; the one pursues the victim, the other strikes it down; the one sells its hide, the other devours the flesh.

And I plied my poesy and said:

Ah, the jackal is turned into a lion,
The righteous kisseth the shoe of the vain.
The workers of deception are robed in dignity,
The evil have attained the upper hand.

He that abominates wickedness must drink the cup
   of poison;
They that wreak evil lord it over him.
His efforts win him no profit;
Though armed with helmet and corselet, they avail
   him not.
They that measure wealth by handfuls
See him descend never to rise.

8

Wolf & Crane

WHOSO SERVES WICKED SINNERS,
HIS REWARD IS ENOUGH IF HE
IS DELIVERED FROM BLOWS.

A WOLF in affliction besought the lion to assemble the
   multitude of his subjects; a large bone had turned
and become lodged in his throat, so that he could not raise
his head. His soul chose strangling, for the bone wounded
him as it pressed upon him in its strait lodgment. All the
cattle and the beasts and the fowl assembled, from the
least to the greatest, and approached the wolf, whom they
found prostrated in his anguish. He sought their counsel
to extract the bone, but they would not respond; "For,"
said they, "this is his cunning; he seeks but a pretext to
destroy us and swallow us alive like the pit. Let us deal
shrewdly and remain unattainted." But when the wolf
continued his pleas, not once or twice but many times,
their hearts melted and turned to water. They all took
counsel together and said with a single voice: "Blessed be
he that did take cognizance of thee! Lo, the crane hath a

long neck and a beak that is strong and sharp and narrow; he will withdraw the bone from its lodgment—who but he can do so? Call him, there is none his equal." So the wolf called the crane and awakened his sympathy (yet the gall of asps was within him), and persuaded him by his speech and vowed to requite him if he would extract the bone and to make him ruler over all that was his. The crane spoke: "Open thy mouth, and I shall see whether I may remove this death from upon thee." So the wolf spread his maw open without measure, and all stood from afar and shrunk back, for they feared to come nigh. The crane grasped the bone between his teeth—for his beak reached down into the throat—and withdrew it; then he asked for his reward. Answered the wolf with harshness: "Who hath heard such a thing, who hath seen it? Am I not the mightiest of the beasts and cattle, and are my fangs not surrounded with dread, and is not the rule of my mouth to rend and destroy? Who hath ever come into my mouth and remained whole? This once hast thou escaped from between my teeth, and I have not strangled thee; twice thy hire have I rendered thee. Depart from me lest I slay thee, lest thy life be for a prey."

The parable is of a rich man whose neighbor does him honor and inclines to his every desire and serves him with all his might. But the master hardens his heart and makes his spirit stern, and if he ask the payment for his service and his toil, he gives it not but works iniquity and scourges his body with rods, and says: "Depart from me! How oft hast thou wearied me! Frowardness hath multiplied among slaves, for they are grown lax and are not disciplined. Make haste, march, do not stand, if thou valuest thy life." So do the shameful ones, men that are harsh and workers of iniquity. But the humble trembles and is afraid; the needy separates from his fellow.

And I plied my poesy and said:

He that relieth upon his wealth and his flocks,
And dealeth with his neighbor as with a slave in his
  tent,
And wickedly works iniquity: when he asketh,
"Give me my hire; I shall gather it and have done,"
He answers, "Quickly begone, depart from my
  boundaries
Ere I thrust thee out"—in the pit shall his lodging be,
Never shall he sojourn in shining light.

9

A Pregnant Bitch & Another

HE WHO MAKES ANOTHER RULE
OVER HIM CARRIES HIM UNTIL
HE BECOME HIS MASTER.

A BITCH yearned to lodge in a house, for her time was
near to whelp and winter was coming on apace.
One evening she approached her fellow whose house and
chamber were in her vicinity and wept and implored her
to hearken to her cry and receive her into her house until
she be released from her travail and her full womb be
disburdened. The other had pity and said: "Lo, my house
is before thee: do as is good in thy sight. Remain while
thy offspring are small until thou hast weaned them." So
the bitch rested there in peace until she whelped puppies
in her own form and image. But the mistress of the house
was displeased, for their yelps rose to heaven, and they
abated not their desires. The puppies grew large and
strong, ate flesh and waxed robust; and as they grew fat
their heart was lifted up and they made of their entrails an

ambush and left no livelihood in the house. Said the mistress to the stranger: "My friend, go forth from my house; depart from me and dwell in thine own abode. Though I love thy nighness we cannot abide together, for thy children give me no peace. The dogs are truculent and vex me sore. Their cry robs me of slumber; woe is me that they sojourn with me so long! They drink my water and eat my bread; my soul is weary of their trouble, and I have no peace at all." The stranger replied with smooth lips: "My honored and upright lady, let my life be given me for my request and my people for my petition. If thou abhor my nighness with thee, do thou send the mother afar but the young shalt thou take for thyself. Then if my offspring and my people say, 'Return to thy mistress and be humbled,' no dog shall raise a cry in thy hearing, and the latter loving-kindness shall be more acceptable than the first. Let me abide until the winter's chill be overpast, and at the time of singing of birds we shall seek another house. Do not bring my old age down to the grave in blood; if my sons be left without shelter at such a season, drought would consume us by day and frost by night. The mercies of the bitch of the house were warmed, and she said: "What is mine is thine, my house is thy house, according to thy request and thy petition." But when the time of the singing of birds came round the stranger and her brood made their hearts adamant. The mistress said in her hearing: "To the right or to the left, go thou and thy sons from my tent. Twice shall affliction not arise. Wherefore wilt thou resolve to repay evil for good?" Then spake the stranger like a robber, and cunningly devised to remove the mistress far from her boundaries. She said to her: "The house is mine. Get thee gone from my place and my demesne. Depart, thou and thy dependents, make haste, begone from my folk." And they hastened to thrust her out. So she departed from her home sorrowing, and the sons of the stranger inherited it. But the shepherds came and drove them forth.

The parable is of a pleasant and complaisant man that is approached by a subverter who works deceit in his house. Cunningly he deludes him with his snares, and in his coming and going ponders deception. He sighs, to lead his patron astray, as if all peace had forsaken his soul, and his eyes pour forth water. The patron's mercies are warmed, so that he fulfills his desires and makes him ruler in his house. He that came as a sojourner betrays him: "Mine is the house and its chambers, and thou art but a guest in my dwelling place." The patron cries out bitterly; if the stranger's society pleased him for a day, he will grieve twice as much on the morrow. And so hath the sage said in his wisdom [Ecclesiastes 7.15]: "There is a just man that perisheth in his righteousness."

And I plied my poesy and said:

The houses of the faithful and their foundations are
    desolate;
In none is there a speaker of truth and uprightness.
The times have silenced and destroyed them; flattery
    and falsehood they have let live.
Righteousness is ended and hidden away and for-
    gotten,
And the righteous have descended to the pit.
But the crooked mount upon a ladder.
Sweet is bitter; light, darkness; stinking water, dew.
The light are esteemed as the weighty; their sin
    illumines their shadow.
If a man approach his friend, he will be paid evil
    for good.
But whoso resists flattery, whoso abides steadfast,
    receives his reward.
He that rendereth evil for good will be blinded;
He shall never behold the light in its splendor.

10

City Mouse & Country Mouse

HE THAT SEEKS GREAT THINGS
WILL BE PLUCKED ON THIS SIDE
AND ON THAT AND WILL CRY OUT
IN BITTERNESS.

A TOWN mouse journeyed from his native place to visit
his kin in another city. All the day he walked, until
evening came on, when he saw a forest nearby in which
country mice were disporting themselves in their soul's
paradise. In this place he lodged with a country mouse in
whom he took pleasure, and each uncovered all his heart
to the other. He observed his food and his drink and how
his hand apportioned them by measure. Their food was
herbs and the like, and the root of the broom. Said he to
the forest mouse: "Thy foot shall follow in my steps; tomorrow shalt thou journey with me and I will make thee
drink of my beverages and thou shalt eat of my viands.
Better for thee will be a day in my courts than a thousand
in the forest midst straitness and oppression, in the blast of
the storm wind, and in lack of food. In winter how wilt
thou find livelihood when the grass is withered? Them
that dwell amongst it it fails, so that they are affrighted
and ashamed. Thou wilt look forth at the windows, but
the grass withereth and the flower fadeth. Come with me
and lift thy head high; I will bestow dainty sweetmeats
upon thy soul." So he enticed him to come from the
forest to the city, a place of wheat and barley, of granaries
and grain. When they came to Bethlehem ["house of
bread"] the city mouse said: "I have compassion upon
thee; lo, all my house is before thee—eat as is thy pleas-

ure." And as they were eating and making merry, with flour and bread and flesh and fish, the man came there as was his wont to fetch bread and supply his board. The city mouse fled and hid in his shelter, and the country mouse hastened after him; so nimble had he not been since his youth. When the man departed thence, the city mouse descended from his cranny and each emerged from the holes where they had lain hidden. The town mouse set his teeth to the corn and the meal and ate and was satisfied and waxed fat; the country mouse kept his distance to see what would befall him that had made himself his companion. He quivered with dread of the man he had seen; his flesh trembled and his spirit was crushed for the path which he had taken, and he repented him of his imaginings. And as the country mouse reflected thus in his heart the city mouse fled from the battlefield and hid him in his place of concealment. Said the country mouse to the town mouse: "Happy he who departs hence in peace and is no longer in fear and dread. From the moment I forsook my lodging the iniquity of my steps has encompassed me. See to thy house and thy place, for I will no longer tarry with thee. Terror has breached our covenant. Come to the rock, hide thee in the dust from before the man, lest he gather thee in his drag, lest the lurker stir from his ambush. All thy life is vexation and wrath; but bread in secret is sweet. Why hast thou slandered the forest? Better a dry crust and tranquillity therewith than a house filled with the sacrifices of contention. From every man that approaches thou fleest in panic and in breathlessness takest refuge in one tent and another. In my place I shall find song and joyful shouting, the beauty of Carmel and Sharon."

The parable is for him who seeks great and wonderful things, who forsakes the good and pleasant and is not content with his lot and his wonted food, but strives to ascend on mounting stairs. Generally he comes to shame; he attains this but loses that, and even the second he contemns. Then he says with lips and tongue: "I shall go and return to my first way, for better for me was it then than now." At times he descends lower and lower, and his cry is bitter, for he is plucked on this side and on that.

And I plied my poesy and said:

Better a dry crust and tranquillity therewith
Than a fatted swan with contention;
Better a handful of meal with love
Than twenty with hatred;
Better a mess of herbs with security
Than venison with contention and greed.
Abide in thy house in peace, and spy not
Another's house with passion flaming and panting.

II

Fox & Eagle

WHOSO INCREASETH HIS
GREATNESS AND WEALTH BY
VIOLENCE WILL IN THE END LOSE
WHAT HE HOLDS MOST PRECIOUS.

A FOX went forth to inspect a garden, his progeny of kits accompanying him. The eagle swooped down and carried one off. The fox perceived that one was missing but knew not whether he had been stolen or was hid, whether he was dead or maimed or captive. He lifted his eyes and saw that the eagle was bearing the kit on his pinions, and he raised his voice and wept and cried out to the eagle: "Deal gently for my sake with my son and return him; thy days will be long if thou preserve him. Wherefore shouldst thou cut off from his kin him thou hast not toiled for nor raised up? Hearken to prudence and knowledge. Wherefore shouldst thou incite evil?" The eagle replied: "Who art thou to spring after me, and what ails thee that thou criest out?" The eagle would not hearken to the fox's voice, and the fox followed along his course. When they came to a tall tree of the forest the fox was filled with fury, for the eagle had cast the kit to the eaglets in his eyrie. When the fox saw that he could not ascend to him he called out: "To cause thee sorrow I shall burn thy tall cedars and thy choice cypresses." So the fox went and set fire to the beams, wool and flax together upon the oaks and the dry timber, and flaxen straw and brittle briars, and piled heaps of logs for a pyre. The fire burned and would not be quenched. As the flame shot out from the wool and flax the fox said: "Let my soul die with the Philistines and my son be consumed with the eagle and his young; before he become food for their fangs let him be destroyed along with them: lo, he is given to the flames to devour." When the eagle saw the great fire he cried a loud and bitter cry and called to the fox: "Take thy son, whose life is precious to thee, and extinguish the fire which thou hast kindled in thy wrath. Wherefore should we die in thy sight?"

The parable is for one who, persisting in his sinfulness, puts his hand forth against his peaceful fellows. He covets and ravins, he robs and plunders. He maketh perfumer's oil to seethe with stench. For that he is strong and rich and powerful he plunders and robs the humble and needy. Even if the poor man address him with words of supplication he stops his ears like an unhearing asp. In the end his secrets break forth, and he too is rendered small in his sight.

And I plied my poesy and said:

The haughty despiseth the humble; the wicked the
   righteous.
But when the humble waxes strong he maketh his
   utterance smooth:
"Account it not unto me for a fault, for I have
   repented;
I shall be to thee as a father, and thou to me as a son."

12

Lion, Goat, Sheep, Cow

HE THAT MAKETH FELLOWSHIP
WITH ONE STRONGER THAN HIMSELF,
IN THE END WILL HIS GLORY BE HUMBLED.

A LION went forth to seek prey, to hamstring it and
   crush the neck, to take game and fetch it home. Accompanying the lordly beast were a goat, a sheep, and a
cow. When they came to the forest they said: "All that
we shall encounter we shall lay low; we shall find prey
and divide it." They saw a hind and took it in their snares,
and they asked the lion to show what portion he desired
to satisfy his need and what each should take for his share.
Now the imaginings of the lion's heart were lofty, and his
right hand was a hammer against the weary; and he said
to them: "Hear my rede: Take not of the flesh; the hind
has fallen to my lot. I found it, and it is wholly mine—the
first portion, because I am king; the second, because I pursued after her and overtook her; the third, because I apportioned the prey, being the mightiest of all my generation; the fourth—but who will stand forth to separate it
from the three? Who will answer me with boldness and

take the prey without my leave? Who is so fierce as to dare stir me, who will stand before me and breach the law my lips have framed?" When they heard his reply they trembled and quaked before him. At each who asked a portion the lion laughed, and rebuked him so that he fled afar. And when they had all dispersed at the sound of his voice, the whole prey was left to him.

The parable is for a man who associates with one stronger than he. If they conclude partnership the richer will roar like a lion and reply in wrath that he hath no portion and inheritance with him. And he shall lose his wealth and his love, either upon that day or its morrow. But the righteousness of the virtuous shall be revealed, even as the sun that goeth forth in his strength.

And I plied my poesy and said:

If a poor man seek the company of the rich,
Portionless will he be driven off, like the lion's
    companions
When, their lots in their bosoms, they asked their
    share.
Quickly, he dispatched them empty-handed, in
    furious rage,
Bearing chaff, not grain. Such his lot who companies
    with one stronger.
Instead of myrrh, rebellion. He sits in folly and walks
    aimless
Who desires to share in power.

13

Crow & Fox

GREAT IS THE POWER OF PRIDE,
EVEN SURPASSING GREED.

A CROW mounted a fig tree, carrying a cheese in his mouth. Under the tree stood a fox, devising and scheming how he might bring the cheese down to earth. He called to the crow: "Stately, handsome, and sweet bird, good and agreeable and lovely, happy is he who is paired with thee. If all the beauties were at thy side their comeliness would not equal thine. If thou shouldst essay to sing songs thou wouldst surpass all birds in music and wouldst be sole perfection, for no flaw is to be found in thee. See whether thy voice matches thy stature and the majesty of thy plumage, for thou art free of fault." The crow said to himself: "I shall let him hear my voice, and he shall heap praise upon praise." So he opened his mouth to raise his voice, whereupon the cheese immediately fell and landed near the head of the fox, who said: "Of the precious things of heaven above this hath come to me from him that raiseth his voice; no longer will I listen to the sound of song." So he went to his own place after he had obtained his desire of the crow.

This parable is for the proud and haughty and for the flatterers and falsifiers who deceive them with their lies and honeyed words, and extract their wealth which they had secreted in vain and in utter futility. Beware, therefore, of the seducer, and be not swayed by the aspect of his figure and the loftiness of his stature; let him not trap thee with his eyeballs, with his false lips, with his violent hands.

And I plied my poesy and said:

A friend hath fooled me; 't is easy to befool a fool;
Easier still it is when one makes himself a fool.

14

Ass, Dog, Man

ENVY BREEDS COVETOUSNESS,
A THING OF VANITY.

IN THE house of a municipal official there lived a small
dog who ate of his bread and slept in his lap, walked
with him and rode with him. In the house an ass lowered,
for that the man was friends with the dog and often played
with him like a pair of gossips. Said the ass to himself: "I
am not inferior to the dog. I too shall approach the master; perhaps he will be friends with me, as with the dog.
I will embrace and kiss him and lick him with my tongue,
I will put my eyes to his, and my face over against his.
And I will be his companion when his friends are by. All
his clothing will I slobber and trample, every shred and
shoe latchet. To win his favor I shall bray at him, just as
the dog frisks and barks. And thus shall I prove whether
I find favor even as the dog." When the master returned
home the ass put his plan into execution. He ran quickly
toward him and licked him about the ears and embraced
him with his forelegs and raised his voice to him and applied his head to his, just as he had learned of the dog. But
the master was stricken with fear, for the ass went up and
down upon him, and hemmed him in with his mouth
until he thrust him from his seat, and he clung to his neck

like a necklace until his weight was heavy upon him. Cried the master: "Hither, all who are with me! Remove the ass from upon me, for his terror is grown great." All the folk assembled, one with a dagger and another with a stick; one pelted the ass with stones and another smote him with a rod; one cried: "Strike, but spare his life." So they chased the ass to his crib, bruised on back and belly.

The parable is for a fickle man whose eyes are broad and whose heart is high; he is lordly in his haughtiness. For such as he there can be no success. In his desire to hold sway he suddenly stumbles and falls and is thrust from his station, and no man heeds his speech. Solomon's proverb remains valid [Proverbs 24.20]: "There shall be no reward to the evil."
And I plied my poesy and said:

Before destruction comes crookedness of ways;
Sloth is a stumbling block on the path to honor.

Recall the man who found a kingdom, and uttered
   prophecy
As he returned from seeking asses.
   [I Samuel, Chapters 9–10]

15

Lion, Mouse, Snare

BETTER TO BE GOOD AND
KINDLY TO ALL, FOR THERE
IS A TIME AND OCCASION
WHEN EVERY CREATURE AVAILS.

A LION was slumbering in a desert place when a mouse
trod upon him and awakened him from his sleep.
He turned to see whose feet had trampled so great a king
as himself, and perceived that the mouse was standing
alone at his side, no creature else. Said the lion, "His time
is come," and called to him: "Vile mouse, thy sentence is
death, for thou hast awakened me and contemned me.
Wherefore hast thou troubled me? It is the frowardness of
thy heart that persuaded thee to tread upon me. But I understand justice: Thou canst not evade me but must pay
the penalty." The mouse replied with heart exceeding
bitter and contrite: "Surely I am innocent and pure. I beseech thee with all my might, let my words find entry
into the ears of my lord, and let not thy wrath kindle
against thy servant. Forget thine anger in thy loving-
kindness. Thou canst perform what thou hast never essayed, but what thou performest thou canst never turn
back. If the heart within thee beats warm, he that con-
fesseth and repenteth will be pardoned. I know that I have

34

behaved foolishly; I have erred, but have not been fro-ward. Who that hath stretched his hand against my lord hath remained guiltless and not come to grief? Far be it from a great and mighty king to put forth his hand to crush a vile mouse." As the mouse spoke thus, the lion's mercies grew warm and he struck a covenant of peace with the mouse. He called to him with kindly lips: "Keep thee, and abide tranquil; fear not."

And it came to pass at midnight, in the midst of thick darkness, at the season of roaring of lions, that the lion was roaring for his prey in a forest and fell into a spread snare. He cried aloud and bitter cry, but when he gathered his strength to rise the snare held him fast. His heart was confounded as his struggles constricted him. At his voice the mouse shook off sleep and went to him and found him entangled from head to foot. He said to the lion: "Who art thou that hath awakened me?" And the lion answered, "Here am I." Said the mouse: "The folk thou hast de-spised—go now and fight in its midst. But the time has come and the season is at hand for my faithful requital of thy good deed. It is in my power to deliver thee from the spread snare even according to the kindness thou didst show me. I shall convoke my fellows to cut the cords of the net and sunder your bonds, so that you may go upon your way prosperous." The lion said to him: "Make haste, good sir; wisdom is better than strength. Thou wilt be more righteous than I if thou wilt bring me forth out of this snare." The mouse assembled his fellows and did as he had said. With their teeth they cut the nets, so that they were severed in an instant. The lion said to him: "Now am I beholden to you, for you have set my feet at large." The mouse turned his shoulder to go upon his way. And the lion returned to his lair unharmed.

The parable is for the poor and humble who are inno-cent of transgression and rebellion in relation with their rich neighbors. If they sin through error and unwittingly, and the rich forgive their error, then when the day of calamity comes upon the rich, the poor strengthen their hands and cleave close to give support, like a girdle to the flesh. There is a friend that cleaves closer than a brother. And there is a man who deals with his brother as on a brazier; he will not deliver his life from the burning. Tried and tested is the sage's saying: "At times a man of giant's stature may be strangled by a fly." A highly esteemed sage was asked: "Whose love is greater, a brother's or a friend's?" And he answered: "Hearken to my words: I do not love my brother until he is also my friend."

And I plied my poesy and said:

> Return the kindness of him who deals kindly with
> thee;
> If he err and do ill, take pity, for it may be on the
> morrow
> He will afford succor in straits, though yesterday he
> were despised.
> Make thy heart humble; circumcise it for the innocent.
> But wither the head of the wicked.

16

Dove & Flax

WHOSO HEEDS NOT COUNSEL,

IN THE END HIS EYE WILL

MINISH AND DROP TEARS.

A DOVE who saw flaxseed strewn upon the ground by the hand of the sower was filled with wrath and said to all the fowl: "Strengthen your weak hands; let none of you be wanting. Let us go forth and eat the seed that wicked man has sown lest it prove our destruction. They that work in fine flax, weave nets to snare winged creatures, whether on the ground or upon branches. My heart is stirred when I behold this sowing, as a reed is stirred in water." For this counsel they said to her: "Not persuasive is the heart of the dove; or her thought is too wonderful for us. Deep it is; who shall plumb it?" And they slandered her, for so was it ordained of heaven. When the dove saw that the birds scorned her words she recounted to her kin and her helpers what the man would do to them and declared that the day of their doom was nigh. Said they: "To understand the report is a vexation." All the kindred foregathered to discover deliverance and enlargement, and each lamented in his heart for the violence which the oppressor prepared. They pleaded with the sower with their tongues, with eloquent discourse; and he said to them: "In the clefts of my house shall ye lie; repose where it seems best to you. If I go to the left or the right, go ye not hither and thither." The doves remained confident in their abodes all the days they tarried there. But of the seed which the man sowed he fashioned gins and every species of snare, and there fell into his snares every manner of bird. But upon that day the doves who heeded the counsel were not for a shame amongst their enemies. They sat in their cotes, and no voice of the pursuer reached them. But those who scorned and mocked the dove were farther astray than she. At the brink of the gaping pit they lamented, and found no resting place for the soles of their feet. Only the doves in the cotes escaped and survived the calamity.

The parable is for one who heeds no counsel; in the end his eye drops tears. In time he perceives that his hand is grown slack; his doom extinguishes the candle of his glory. He will say: "My heart and my eyes have vexed me, for I heeded not the voice of my teachers." And the sages, whose heart within them is wise, have said [Proverbs 12.15]: "The way of the fool is right in his own eyes, but he that hearkeneth unto counsel is wise."

And I plied my poesy and said:

Uncircumcised are the ears of the fool;
His heart is empty of understanding.
He is not warned by the admonishing voice;
Hence will it come about that he fall and rise not.
But the wary perceives the evil, and hides
When the many are suddenly overtaken.
Woe worth the day Gedaliah son of Ahikam
Refused to heed Johanan son of Kareah!

17

Cicada & Ant

REMOVE THE HEDGE OF SLOTH,
AND THINE EYES SHALL NOT
LOOK AND LANGUISH.

A CICADA approached an ant to ask food of her, for she was in sore need of provision for the winter. But the ant turned her back and scorned her speech and mocked her. Said she: "Thine end is sorrow. Whom dost thou pass in beauty? In the summer thou didst slumber and hast prepared no food for the winter. How foolish of heart he that would give thee what he hath stored up! Know that my hand is too short for thee. What didst thou in harvest time? The hay appeareth and the tender grass showeth itself; all the folk go forth to glean, each diligent to prepare for the winter. The sluggard sayeth, 'There is a lion in the streets.' He that wishes to store up grain must collect ears, even as I, who bore them upon my shoulder and prepared my bread in summer." The cicada replied: "All the season of birdsong, when the wagon was loaded with sheaves, I learned to sing pleasant songs and enlarged my fellowship and chased sorrows from my heart, for the songs were true in my sight, and they said my voice was sweet. But now drought hath consumed me, and the chill of winter's ice is vexatious to me." Said the ant: "Now will granary and winepress give you no help, because you have taught your voice song and have taken no thought for food. If thou makest thy nest in the cedars and thy neck comely with chains, go to the house of a rich man; make your music fine and multiply your songs, to fill your soul when you are hungry. To me your words are an abomination. Depart from me, begone! All the men of my counsel abhor thee. Because I am of lowly stature and have no strength or power I have filled my tent with good things. But if I have been wise, I have been wise for myself. But you will not be sustained by song when the northerly blasts blow, for slumber is clothed in tatters, and sluggishness begets deep sleep."

The parable is for a man too slothful to find provision for his house; will others then heed his cry? In the summer he slumbers and sleeps. Such a man is accounted guilty.
And I plied my poesy and said:

Be diligent, my son; cross road and city in the heat
of day;
Gather for the winter, garment and steed, ox and
sheep,
But all in innocence. Pierce the fool's right eye,
Muzzle his mouth, break his teeth.

18

Raven & Sheep

CHANGE NOT WHAT IS THINE UNTIL
SOME OTHER FALL TO THY LOT.

A RAVEN perched upon a sheep's back. Now hear what
she did: She pulled and plucked the fleece from his
back. Said the sheep: "Raven, depart from me. Hear my
words and my discourse; so will you do if you possess
understanding. Go and perch upon the back of the dog,
and pluck his wool from his back, leaving him only bare
skin." Said the raven: "Not so. Thou counselest me for
thine own behoof. Thy wool have I found first, and here
shall I sit, for I delight in it. My counsel is better than thy
counsel. I shall not change nor substitute the dog for thee."

This parable is nigh unto my palate. The cat knoweth
whose beard he licks. He that offers counsel unasked is
reckoned a tedious fool, for to give counsel to one who
loathes it, is wrong.

And I plied my poesy:

Give counsel to him that asks, but let secrets remain
hidden.
Be strong and of good courage in thy lot, and thou
shalt not encounter the froward.

19

Two Deer

A FOOL THAT IS SILENT IS
RECKONED WISE, AND SITS
AMONG THE UNDERSTANDING.

TWO DEER stood in the fields conversing in a hushed whisper though there was none to overhear. Each put his ear to his fellow's lips to catch his words. A passer-by came upon them and proceeded to inquire why they spoke their counsel in a whisper, since there was none to interpret, and even if they should shout with all their strength none could understand their conversation, for they were remote from man. They answered: "We are constrained to make our sweet counsel together, and neither of us reveals his secret. This is our usage for that we are weak."

The parable is for fools that are silent or whisper to one another; then people say, "They are exceeding wise." But when their counsel is revealed, then is their wisdom shown brutish. And so hath the Preacher declared in his proverbs [Proverbs 14.18]: "The simple inherit folly." And the sage hath said: "Better to endure a fool in all his concerns than to endure a fool who is wise in his own sight."
And I plied my poesy and said:

Be wise, my son; and discern and know;
Acquire truth and cultivate innocence.
Reckon a fool as the shadow of an idol,
And turn aside from the counsel of the simple.
If he bids build, then destroy;
Turn to him who understands the matter.

20

Eagle, Snail, Raven

THEY THAT ARE SHREWD
IN CUNNING COUNSEL
ARE WISER THAN HUMANKIND.

A SNAIL went his innocent way, his house with him
wherever he went, for he carried it upon his back.
His head and torso emerged; and his horns, which grew
from it, stood upright as he came forth. When an eagle
soared before the snail he became aware of it and lowered
his horns, and his heart was vigilant for fear—the prudent
hides when he sees evil. The snail quickly hid himself in
his tent, in the upper chamber which was his. The eagle
saw that the snail was hidden and gone, but the path to his
privates could not be seen. He neared the tent and overturned it and perceived that what he had first observed
was there hidden in its resting place. He raised the house
upon his pinions and declared that the snail would not
escape from within before he worked his will upon it.
And as he bore it between heaven and earth he essayed to
breach its shell and crush it with beak and talons, but saw
that he could not penetrate it. Before him stood a raven,
who drew ever nearer and called to the eagle: "Sense hath
betrayed thee. Lo, thou seest with thine eyes but thou
shalt not eat of it. Why rouse thy wrath for this? The battle is not to the strong. Who shall open the doors of his
face? He is proud in his scaly armor, which is molten like
stone upon his back. He that made him can reach him
with His sword. Not thine is the science of piercing him;
it is hidden from the fowl of heaven except only me, who
am now come, and am wise and expert. The prey attached
to thee is exceedingly desirable; if thou give me a share

and portion thou wilt break it like the crushing of a crock and see what is cunningly concealed within; then wilt thou know the paths of his house." Answered the eagle: "After that thou hast bruised the enigma's head just are the terms thou hast stipulated. Teach me to remove the covering, and receive a share alike with mine." Said the raven: "Go up to the strong cliff; its descent thence will crush it. Cast it to the ground as with a sling, and thou shalt shatter it upon the rock. The shell will be powdered to dust, and then canst thou eat the flesh." The eagle heeded this counsel, and cast the snail from the cliff down to earth. But before it left his hand the raven went to the foot of the cliff, and there he found the snail shattered and scattered. He devoured it, leaving not a morsel. The eagle grieved sore for having heeded the raven's counsel, for his own prey he had made ready for the raven; his cunning had made him release his booty; and he had cast food away from his teeth.

The parable is very pleasing: Better is wisdom than warrior gear, and the shrewd and clever can by their counsel destroy what the sons of men have builded. Though a man be confident in the strongholds he has made and in his towers, his enemies may devise cunning schemes against him. Wisdom must have a smooth path in his heart, lest their cunning overreach him, as did the raven's the eagle.

And I plied my poesy and said:

A man wars upon his neighbor for wealth, and defeats him;
But a passing stranger gathers it up in his skirts—
Like a bone over which two dogs fight,
But a third comes and seizes.

21

Wolf & Goats

THEY THAT MULTIPLY WORDS
HARDEN THEIR HEARTS, AND IN
THEIR MIDST LURKERS SET SNARES.

A GOAT raised her kids in the flock, surrounded by a house with wall and hedge. When the man rose early to his ploughing the goat would seek all manner of herbage and spy out pasturage in the hills. Said she to her buck: "Know that my grazing is far hence; I shall not return until I have filled my belly and my bare bowels to provide milk in plenty for my kids. Shut the door upon thee, and hide; depart not until I return. Put not thy hand forth to open the door until thou see me before thee; then will I show thee all my good things." The buck replied, saying: "We shall go together and feed and watch." So the twain went together. A small kid they left behind they bade fasten the door, and she locked it after them, and the house was barred to entry. Now the wolf was lurking in his lair, crouched for destruction, his reins yearning to attack the flock and ravage it, to seize prey and devour it. He knew that the goat and buck were not there, nor yet their master the man. So he disguised himself and his voice simulated that of the kid's mother, and he said: "Open for me, for the milk I bring thee in my udders is abundant. I am weary of grazing, and they cannot carry more food." The kid answered: "The voice is the voice of my mother, but I fear that it is not my kin that stands behind our wall. In the forest are they that lurk for us; I shall not open until eventide because of the lurking wolf, lest my mother be transformed into a stranger and the wolf destroy me in my vale of peace. Let not the men of my counsel declare that

44

with me is fulfilled the prophecy: 'The wolf shall dwell with the lamb, and the leopard shall lie down with the kid.' " The wolf perceived that his words would not avail, so he said: "If thou open not I will bring thee down in sorrow to the grave. For that thy heart is filled with violence I will break thy walls and thou shalt be trampled down. With my blade I shall make an opening in thy door." Said the kid: "Let not him that girds on the sword boast as one who has opened. Neither by suasion nor by anger nor by deception wilt thou enter here with me."

The parable is for men whose hearts and words are harsh, the rebellious and lying folk who wrap themselves in fringed mantles in order to deceive at the gate. Each neglects his own labor, for deception, and in time of trouble they dissemble. They speak with two hearts; though they display love in their dealings, there is falsehood in their right hand. If he that dwells amongst them is not their like, if his heart be not false midst their false hearts and deceive not with their deception, if he prepare not his refuge within him and devise not shifts against cunning shifts and guile against guile, he will not survive amongst them save through a miracle; for the evil are at peace and the good, humbled; the false, upstanding and the faithful, tottering.

And I plied my poesy and said:

Berechiah's house departs from the men of falsehood
    and is not taken,
Even as seven stars disperse at the cock's crowing.

22

Serpent & Rich Man

HE THAT REPAYETH EVIL FOR
GOOD, HIS SOUL INCURRETH DEBT.

A SERPENT moved freely in a rich man's domain; regular commons were provided for him by the rich man when he came, and milk to quench his thirst. One day the rich man was stirred so that his lips were filled with fury; he raged, and cursed his people and his house and his comrades. The serpent came as was his wont to obtain his supply in the house, and his foot fingered the rich man's face. He smote the serpent in anger, for he escaped not his wrath; and the serpent returned to his house bruised and smitten and downcast. Calamity twofold had befallen him, and he was no more seen in the rich man's domain or its approaches.

And it came to pass in the course of time that the rich man was wonderfully debased. His wealth vanished, and poverty overtook him; his cattle and all his wealth perished, and his cares grew ever heavier. Instead of barley there was noisomeness; the path of his destruction was paved smooth, and his hand availed not to deliver. Said he: "It is for my transgression that I am stricken. Yesterday the serpent was in my house, and in my anger I bruised him though he committed no violence or deception. I shall go and seek his face in his tent; perhaps he will be appeased and I may prevail upon him with persuasion and smoothness of tongue to return to his former habit." So he came to the serpent and lamented and wept before him and implored him to banish his hatred against him and not kindle all his wrath. So said the man, weeping: "Serpent, hear my rede: Though thou art angry with me,

46

return, and I shall supply all thy requirements. Thou knowest that I love thee and that I befriended thee in my house and that my affection protected thee so that thou hast lacked nothing. If in my anger I smote thee, lo, in my benevolence I had compassion upon thee. Bear now the transgression of the bruise, and I shall be your willing servant." In reply the serpent said: "I will not requite a man according to his former deeds, for the blows I received afflicted me so sore I had near killed a man for my bruise. Let not my hearers be astonished; all thy household know that dread of me did not affright thee. Wherefore persist in thy pleading? I shall no more return to thy house; I do not long for thy dainties. Thou hast wounded my head and breached the palisade of peace to raise thy sword against me; if today thou laugh, tomorrow I will make thee sad. Thou shalt not rejoice at the sight of the death thou hast brought upon me. I shall not visit thy sin upon thee nor be vigilant for thy evil; yet whenever I recall and behold, my bruise is sore and my heart, anguished, and a fire smolders in my nostrils. Depart, lest I slay thee in my wrath, for the pain is strong upon me and my wound is exceeding heavy. If not, I will remember thy sin in fury and thy heart will study dread of my elder son, the viper. For out of the serpent's root shall come forth a cockatrice, and his fruit shall be a fiery flying serpent which shall encompass thee to avenge me. At his sudden rebuke thou shalt be astonied and unstrung."

The parable is of a man who deals frowardly with his friend to do him ill in his hatred, though he be not an enemy or one that wished him ill, but dwelt with him secure and did him and his house no harm. But by reason of the evil he inflicted upon him he sowed the seed of enmity in his heart, to be harvested when occasion offered, for the friend sees that his day must come. His requital is twofold: If the culprit do not pay the penalty, the kindred of his flesh who know his nature will do so. He never despairs of wreaking his vengeance, with furious rage and flaming fire. Therefore should the worker of evil not be astonished if one that received evil at his hands is filled with wrath against him. His hands bring his doom near, and he is harassed in all his ways. He will rejoice in his misfortune and instigate it. Blind is he who puts trust in a man he has injured. And the sage hath said: "He that governeth not his anger, how shall he govern another?" My heart inclineth to the saying: "He that soweth hatred reapeth regret."

And I plied my poesy and said of them that make light darkness and sweet bitter:

> Berechiah has inscribed with his pen:
> Who soweth hatred will reap regret;
> He inflicts a gash upon himself,
> Fashions it with a graving tool.
> Who bruises his fellow or plucks his hair
> Whets a sword against himself.
> If the way of his enemy is perverse
> He will gather the gleanings of his hatred.

23

Lion & Fox

HE THAT HIDES IN AN EVIL
TIME WILL NOT FEAR TIDINGS.

IN THE dead of night and deep darkness a lion pondered and reflected, and a wicked plan took form. The lion said in his heart: "Every king sits in his house at ease, and why do I toil, my soul in want, a wanderer and a vagabond in search of food? Nothing comes into my mouth except by chance encounter. Why do I labor in vain and exhaust my body in struggle and find no peace? Who of all my servants takes pity upon me? Better is a handful of quiet than heaping handfuls of toil." Guilefully he published abroad that he was sore ill, and with smooth and lying lips he summoned the cattle and the beasts: "Make haste and come to see me, for I know not the day of my death. There is none to plead my cause that I may be bound up and healed. I shall scatter among you riches and spoil; your wants I shall satisfy, and I shall give even as you bid me. I will render to each according to his righteousness; for the greater, I shall increase his heritage. If not now, when? Lo, I shall sleep with my fathers." They journeyed all to visit him, great and small. And it came to pass, when there was yet a league to go, that they were told of the king's injunction and its reason: Visitors must come singly and not two at once to visit such an invalid as he, lest their voices disturb him. So they went each one alone, and found the lion lying upon his side in his lair as one dead. Said the visitor: "Truly, my lord, to behold thy welfare have I hurried my steps." Answered the lion: "What hast thou to do with my welfare? Turn thou behind me. Full oft hast thou wearied me; now shalt thou be shamed for seven days. Thy flesh will I eat and thy bones crush; the fleet shall not escape, nor the strong deliver himself." And the lion did according to his words; he rent him in pieces and devoured his flesh. While he was yet eating another came and said: "My lord king, of thy sickness is my flesh wracked." The lion enticed him into his lair by the smoothness of his tongue and did unto him as he had done unto the first. So fared also the third, and also all that followed after the flocks. The lion stirred not thence until they were dismembered; and so fared all until they were ended. There remained only the fox, who pondered in his heart to know and understand what the king sought in his heart, and what would be done to him, for it was not explained. His heart fainted, for he trusted not what was said among the peoples, that the king would give fields and vineyards to all. And if the truth were with them, why had he enjoined his servants not to come to him, two together? "I shall not go," said the fox, "lest I fall into a gin and a snare." And he went and sate him afar off, two bowshots' distance, and he hid him alone in a secret place to hear the bleatings of the flocks, and he said: "I observe the adder goeth as a wind goeth and returneth not; lo, they all go with no fear, but not one returns. I know not what it means; it is the manner of Jehu [who came unto them and came not again]. Their path is like a slippery way in the darkness; surely the king cheateth them, and they will never return to their homes. Calamity will befall those who expected to see his calamity; they will not eulogize him, 'Alas for our lord, alas for his majesty!' " And because the fox's heart was fearful and vigilant, shrewdly he hid him when he perceived evil. And it came to pass when the lion had finished rending all comers, that he understood that the fox had cleverly hidden himself, and he called out: "Why and wherefore do thy footsteps tarry? Surely thou hast put forth thy hand against thy comrades." Answered the fox: "The way of those going I saw, but I found no footsteps of those returning."

The parable—so say they that speak in parables: The pressure of the times is fortune's wheel. When a wondrous thing comes about, each man seeks his own welfare. Remain each man where he is; let none go forth from his place. The news is not good; the evil report multiplies. But there is one who hides, in the day of wrath, and fears no evil tidings. Enough the trouble, in its own time, when it reaches thee, and there is destruction in thy tent.

24

Frogs, Oak, Serpent

WHO DWELLETH SECURE IN HIS
OWN WORLD ACQUIRES NO MASTER
OVER HIMSELF.

FROGS consulted amongst themselves to set a king over them. On the question—Who should be king?—they disagreed; one said so, and another so, until they all agreed that the king over them should be a tree planted upon streams of water, whose height reached heaven. They said unto the tree: "Rule over us; thou hast a garment; be thou our chief." The tree was silent and uttered not a word, but the voice of their multitude prevailed and they said all with a single breath: "Our lord the king live forever!" They reached their desired haven, and joy beat strong in their hearts. From the first day of his reign the oak began to look upon the fruits of the valley. One came to the king and another returned, but there was neither hatred nor love. From the day they made him king they made pilgrimage to him, to sit beneath his shadow. They knelt and bowed down to him and said: "Our lord the king, we have come to thee. Who is like thee in stature? Our souls long for thy words. Look down from thy holy mansion for the benefit of thy servants, lead them and teach them the good way, for love covereth all transgression." They called to him in a loud voice but there was neither sound nor response. Then said they all: "Lo, if thou wilt not tell us thy name all we frogs will turn aside from thee."

And when they saw that he told not his secret they exchanged his glory for shame and plotted to separate from him. And they said: "Not good is his timber and not good, his leaves. If evil come upon the land the fixed spike shall not budge; from him issueth neither tears nor laughter." Therefore did they transgress the law and change the statute. But he was plagued by God and smitten with blindness. All the flocks assembled there to call him The Oak of Weeping, for the majesty of royalty beseemed him not, for that his heart was like flint and stirred not from its place. Verified was the proverb on the lips of the multitude: "All that are tall are fools." "From the day this one reigned over us," said they, "our people have become a lowly folk; their aspect is diseased, as in the beginning." They trampled him with their feet and wearied of his being king over them, and they spewed upon him and made of him a jakes. One said: "Lo, I have seen a chieftain for us; we will forsake the bramble and choose the cypress." And they said: "No bruised reed shall rule over us, neither bramble nor cypress. We shall not regard his tall stature nor his appearance. There is no breath in his nostrils; what is his worth? We shall choose a king terrible and awful, one that is alive as we are this day, who will fight our battles and speak with us mouth unto mouth." So they chose for their king the serpent, who heeds no enchantment. He joined their band as a comrade, and his society was approved by them. Frog and snake walked in company, shoulder to shoulder, so that no breeze came between them. But one day when he was with them and the waters were calm the serpent grew famished and became angry, and he said to them: "Be ye humble at my hand; do ye come to search me out?" And he smote them a great smiting, and maligned them, and hated them yet more, and devoured their flesh and their bones, until all that were in the rivers perished. He gathered them in great heaps and devoured ten portions, from the houses and the fields. Better for them it were to be without overseer and ruler than to multiply destruction in their camps.

The parable is for the sons of man in whose power it lies to abide peaceful in their houses, but they conspire in their schemes and their inward plottings and an evil thing sprouts among them, so that their peace is banished, as befell the frogs. And the sage hath said: "The king is likened to a fire, in which thou hast no hope; in storm thou hast need of it, but if thou draw nigh it will burn thee."

25

Sheep, Ram, Lion

BE NOT FOR A MOCKERY AND
A JEST WHEN THOU SEEST THY
WORDS FIND NO FAVOR.

SHEEP were left in the fold when the shepherds went
forth where they listed and shut not the door behind
them. They were far from man, and all went forth from
their fold to spy out their food in the fields. The sheep
grazed as is their wont, scattered here and there, and their
sweet counsel was to eat grass. They had not gone far
from the fold when a lion journeying toward the forest
gathered his strength to pursue them. When they became
aware of him one called to another: "The lion hath
roared; who shall not be afraid?" When they saw that the
lion would charge them and their escape was lost they
said to the ram who marched at their head: "Go toward
the lion on the course he is taking and appease him with
smooth speech. Mayhap he will be appeased and depart
from against us." So the ram journeyed forth from his
host and set his face toward the wilderness. Before he
neared the lion he cajoled the beast with blandishments,
saying to him: "My lord the king, blessed art thou in thy
coming; thou shalt find festival in the eyes of all that behold thee." Answered the lion: "The festival which I shall
find will proceed from thee and thy fellows. What greeting can there be between me and thee? Forbear thy pleasant discourse. Shall a king like me be informed by the
words of thy mouth? There is no joy but in thy flesh,
which I shall eat; for the words of thy mouth I shall not
praise thee."

54

The parable is for one who sees a day of trouble, but his purse and its contents are precious in his eyes, so that he gives no ransom for his soul but thinks to escape with goodly words and soft and smooth speech. But all his words kindle fire and compass sparks; he shall not escape in the day of wrath. But pleasant shall it be for another, who shall say: "Take this host and plunder its gold." He has heaped on silver, but they shall not slander him, for in time of trouble his head is high. All that a man hath, he shall give for his life.

26

Ass, Bees, Wasp

SCORN NOT ANYTHING, FOR THERE
IS A TIME FOR EVERYTHING,
AND OCCASIONS ARE EXIGENT.

A N ASS was grazing upon a hill, surrounded by a swarm of bees. Before him hovered a wasp, until it hid in one of his ears. It shook and trembled and roused him with its buzz as it stormed about hither and thither. The ass was wearied of his life and startled, for he was bitten and stung. He was sore vexed and greatly pained by the noise of the great tumult, and he said: "Today my torments are increased; what is the sound in my ears? Surely it is an ill wind. If thou art within my boundary, wasp, wherefore hidest thee in my cranny? Come forth and do battle with me, that we may look upon one another face to face. Hast thou strength and power to go forth and muster a swarm of bees to battle with a company of asses?" Answered the wasp: "Would that it were so, that we might fight together in the valley, battle line against battle line, wasp against ass and ass against wasp, with the vanquished banished from the congregation." Answered the ass: "Let us appoint a day on which we shall go forth to battle." So the day was there appointed. The ass went to take counsel of the lion who ruled over them all, and told him all that had befallen—of the wasp in his ear that had stung him, of the battle day appointed, and how his heart abode in terror lest the wasp again invade his ear. Said the lion: "Give ear, I will counsel thee. Hearken to my voice, and no plague or pain shall befall thee. With leathern strips stop up and seal all thy perforations; then will not thine enemies prevail over thee. When they see this they will be confounded before thee, and thou shalt hold sway over them but they shall not hold sway over thee. Set thy face toward the battle, and gird thy loins." All the asses did so, and on the day appointed they came, archers and marshals, and the wasps fought against them. But when they saw that every opening was blocked, front and rear, they hid under the belly and there displayed their prowess and inflicted twofold affliction upon the asses. The asses countered by scratching against trees and brush and sought to slay the wasps, until their bonds broke and their holes and crevices were revealed. These did the wasps then enter with vigor, and bit and stung and harassed. The asses were breached from end to end, their ambush within them, and their hearts were overwhelmed with weariness. Said they to the wasps: "We shall no longer be headstrong and rebellious. Lo, we are thy slaves; only depart from us."

The parable is for one who boasts of his stature and his large limbs; the little man rules over him by clever devices. Therefore make not thy flesh to sin with thy tongue, saying to the little man, "My little finger is thicker than thy loins," for many have stumbled and been crushed by excess of pride. No battle is good save the battle against lust.

27

A Planted Tree & Reeds

THE SIN OF PRIDE IS HARD AS
CEDAR; THE QUALITY OF HUMILITY
SOFT AS A REED.

A TREE stood planted in courses of water, but the storm-wind blasted it once and again and uprooted it and overturned it and cast it upon the river, so that it wandered and was tossed hither and yon, even as the reed is bent, and the waves and the breakers passed over it; but the reed and the sedge that were there, were strangers to it. It said to them: "How have I fallen while ye withstand the wind that hath laid me low? Tell me if ye know." They answered: "If thou hadst yielded to him as do we and hadst bowed down, thou hadst not been thrust from thy post. Of all the host of reeds the wind hath felled not one, for he hath found them with heads bowed, as in the swamp."

The parable is for the haughty with neck outstretched. Double destruction is their lot. When the feet of the humble stand fast, sorrow afflicts the proud. Therefore, where there is no man, endeavor thou to be a man. Be thou lowly without vileness and stately without haughtiness.

And I plied my poesy and said:

The words of the proud man are without substance;
Who would stand in his lot?
The dust of his feet is of equal worth with himself;
Why then be slave to his shadow?

28

Mouse, Sun, Cloud, Wind, Wall

IF A MAN PURSUES AFTER HONOR
AND DOMINION, QUICKLY WILL
THEY FLEE FROM HIM.

A MOUSE said in his heart: "Of what sort is a male without a wife? I have seen all living things and all flesh,
but among all these I have not found a woman." His soul
was eager to search and seek out a beautiful woman, one
of goodly favor—white tinged with red—who tasted no
food, and who, when he turned his shoulder to go forth,
would not go forth with him. But in all his speculation he
found no woman without fault, but only the sun perfect
in beauty. And he said: "If the heavens are darkened for
all the dwellers of earth, the sun abides righteous and bears
healing on its wings." And when the sun shone before
him she won favor and grace in his eyes, and he said to
her: "With an everlasting love have I loved thee; therefore have I drawn thee after me and will betroth thee unto
me for a wife. Mine is the right of redemption and inheritance." The sun answered with guile: "Dost thou reckon
this wisdom, to take thee a light which darkened yester-
eve? The sun rises and the sun sets; thine eyes look dark-
ling upon it, and it is gone. Ever doth the cloud conceal it,
for lo, I am a bounden handmaiden to the cloud, for by its
will I am clothed with portions of darkness. But take thee
a wife from thy mother's kindred and her birthplace."
But he stood fast and said: "I do not wish to take such."
The sun said: "Then lift your eyes to the cloud. I know
that she will not turn her face from thee." The mouse's
loins yearned to go to the cloud straightway, and he said
to her: "This day have I labored and found my beloved,

58

my beauteous one, my perfect one; by the sun's counsel I take thee, and I will never forsake thee." The cloud answered and said: "He that watches upon the height of heights placed me in the power of the wind, who shifts me according to her will, north and south, east and west, with outstretched arm and mighty strength. If thou desirest a wife like me, thou wilt be a wanderer and a vagabond upon the earth. Forsake the handmaiden and take the mistress, for I am delivered over to the power of the wind. Go to the wind and prosper with her; you will persuade her and win her over. Go thou and so do." So the mouse went to the wind, whom he found in a desert land, and said to her: "Be not ashamed; with me, my bride, thou shalt come forth from Lebanon, for of all the women I have beheld for myself, thee have I seen before me in this generation. No other wife shall I take beside thee; thou shalt be mine and I thine." She answered him: "Now hast thou come to take me, but thou knowest not my lowliness. In me there is no strength or force to raze a wall—whether of stone or of sand—by my shout. Thy covenant with me shall be voided, for the wall is stronger than I. If she is suitable in thy sight and thou availest to persuade her, she shall be thy fortress in time of stress." So he went to the wall and said: "Know that I have come to thee by the counsel of Sun and Cloud and Wind to visit thee for happiness, and I shall betroth thee unto me with lovingkindness and mercy." The wall answered in anger: "To demonstrate my shame and disgrace have they sent thee unto me, to make me a mockery. Thou hast come to me to rehearse my shortcomings, for they ascend and descend, whereas my stones and sand never budge and no power or strength is in me. Every mouse and creeping thing mines at my source and uncovers my foundation and makes paths upon me. I am a wall and my breasts are as towers, but the mice according to their families chip me with mouth and foot and sojourn in me, mother and sons, in more than two hundred warrens, and I cannot withstand them. Wilt thou desire such a wife as I?" When the mouse saw that his enterprise was betrayed he took him a wife of his own kindred, who was born in his own neighborhood and vicinity, and he found her a proper helpmeet.

The parable is for one who pursues honor to attain it, but dominion and glory flee from him. Whoso exalts himself beyond his proportions is destined to return to his vile origins, for each returns to his own station, the honorable to honor and the lightly esteemed to his own sort. The Arab sage hath said: "Whoso dyes his hoariness will be betrayed by the growing of his hair." And of one who goeth up without permission Solomon hath said [Proverbs 25.7]: "Better it is that it be said to thee, Come up hither."

And I plied my poesy and said:

With head bowed and heart contrite and eye lowly, feet stand fast.
Behold, the fire which rises sinks, and waters minish and stand still.

29

Crow & Other Birds

HE THAT BOASTETH OF WHAT IS NOT HIS,
THE SPIRIT OF FOLLY STIRS IN HIM.

THE CROW thought his nature ill, for his appearance was darker than black and his feathers were like pitch, whereas all other birds have beautiful feathers, red and white and golden and green. Hence it was that all birds whistled at him in scorn, for he was blacker than them all. So he sighed and turned his back, and in his reins conceived a plan: He would take a single feather, no more, from every bird, and go into a secret place there to cast his plumage and in its place assume another which should be compounded of all colors and make him more beautiful than all his peers. This plan he carried out to the full. To the highroad he then ran, up the path, quickly in the joy of his heart, and his feathers were of mottled colors. There he preened himself on his colorful plumage. His fellows gathered about him, and a mixed multitude attended them, and they all sat about him and wondered who and what he might be, for among the agreeable sorts there was none like him. But his stature was the stature of a crow, and when they examined his form each recognized his own feather. This one said, This is my feather, and that one said, This is my feather; this one said, Thou hast vexed me, and this one plucked out his feather, and this one scratched his body, so that he remained naked and plucked, for he had made his way perverse.

The parable is for a man who adorns himself with what is not his. If he hears a wise saying he says he thought it in his own heart; but when he is asked counsel he is silent as a stone. Some there are who give chaff in the place of grain. As a result of his wisdom a man will go bowed down, for instead of wheat he puts forth briars. Better to be a silent fool than to be wise in one's own esteem. If he open his mouth he will reveal his folly, and all will laugh at his counsel. Many have extinguished the light of their glory and paved the path of their doom.

30

Ox, Lion, Ram

WHO HATH A LURKING ENEMY SHALL
TREMBLE MORNING AND EVENING.

An ox saw a lion and ran away, for the lion roared and bellowed and trumpeted after him, and he hid him in a certain pit beneath thick flaxen cordage, where a ram was hidden. His heart's terror made him tremble in fear of the ram. Said the ram to him: "Why art afraid? Surely thou and I belonged to the same herd." The ox answered: "Every animal I see alive is in my eyes a mighty lion. If I had found thee alone I had not feared thee, but now because of the lion I am confounded and atremble."

The parable is for a man that has an enemy whom he fears always, morning and evening, walking and sitting, rising and lying down. Every man he imagines is his enemy, and says, Now shall I be pursued; but it is the sound of a driven leaf that pursues him.

31

Young Dog & Old Dog

WHOSO BOASTS OF HIS ELOQUENCE
IS UNWITTING OF HIS EVIL.

A man had a little dog that snapped at every creature. He hung a bell upon the dog's neck to make a loud sound which was heard when the dog ran, so that he might no longer bite without warning. From the day he wore the bell, the dog's heart was uplifted; he arose as a young lion, and as a lion comported himself. He imagined he was king over the dogs, and walked proudly with neck outstretched. An old dog looked upon him and raised his voice against him, saying: "Why art thou proud of the bell thou showest? It is not for thy benefit or thy delight but to warn against thy wickedness folk thy teeth bite and rend. Therefore let thy words be few."

The parable is for a man who treads his bow for false speech. He searches out the faults of his neighbors, but his own ambush is strong within him. He goes forth in the street to speak, and the ruler of the city shares his counsel and makes him govern his domain, though he know him a slanderer and a sycophant. Proudly he lords it over the humble in his vicinity, but he knows that it is not for his own merits.

32

Cock & Hen

WISDOM MEET FOR A TIME
OF RECKONING IS BETTER
THAN ANY CHOICE VESSEL.

A COCK said to his hen: "There is no more wheat or cars; wherefore are we laggard? There is famine in the city and we shall die. Let us go and lodge in the villages. My brother hath a granary of barley, and there shall we dwell for a whole year, about the granary and its plenty." The two went forth together and walked a day's journey until they came to the city in a land of wheat and barley. There the hen built her nest, and before the year's end there were chicks in her form and image, seven robust cockerels and a puny, ailing pullet. When she clucked to her brood, they scratched for grain with their feet as did she. They ate share and share alike; there was abundance, and the mother rejoiced in her offspring. When the time of harvest came, they spoke of returning to the place of their own dwelling, and the cock said: "Give ear. We shall not return to our folk empty-handed, lest we be for a mockery in their eyes, as if we had come from a place of famine. Rejoice and be glad at my saying. Look upon me and do ye likewise. Each one—cock, chick, and hen—shall carry an ear of corn in his mouth, until ye come to the land of wheat; and ye shall bring forth the old before the new." Said the hen: "Thy counsel is good and sound. Give a portion unto seven, yea unto eight, and each shall carry an ear in his mouth." The eighth was unequal to the burden, for he was sickly; this is what befell him: As they walked by the way of the wilderness, their band in confusion, a fox lay hidden in the forest thickets and watched the band as it came on. The cock was aware that it was upon him and all his host that the fox cast his eye, and he said: "Trembling hath seized me, and my heart is confounded. She that hath borne seven is waxed feeble. The apprehensions of this ambush terrify me, lest he come and smite me, mother upon children. But let us plot cunningly how we may escape, lest he be master over us as he was master over our fathers, for ever is he guileful toward us." As the cock was yet speaking the lurker emerged from the covert where he had lurked, and approached the sickly one and said: "Whose are these and what do they carry in their mouths?" He answered: "The tails of foxes are they carrying, which they wrested from the foxes by their strength, and then flayed the skin from upon them." The fox said: "If such are their deeds, why then is your mouth not laden as is theirs?" And he answered: "It is for this that thou hast come toward me, for it is *thy* tail that I await. Thou shalt no more return to thy tent; my lot I shall make fall upon thee." When the fox heard this he ran away, as the strong man runs a course.

The parable is for a man whose garments are tattered and whose words are not heard. In the assembly of the rich he is for a mockery, and his timely wisdom is despised. But at the day of reckoning the wisdom that issues from his mouth is better than any precious vessel.

33
Brazen Pot & Clay Pot

WHOSO WISHES TO SWALLOW
ONE THAT IS RICHER THAN HE
WILL DISCOVER THAT HE CANNOT
VIE WITH HIS SUPERIOR.

TWO POTS, one of copper and one of earthenware, looked upon one another as they floated on the water. The clay pot envied the copper, for it was clothed in scarlet, and said to her: "How canst thou be proud in thy much praise, for that thou art styled polished brass? Though thou glisten like gold, mine is twice thy strength to fare speedily over the face of the water. I can run two miles twice ere thou run a mile. Because of thy ponderous weight thou lovest repose. It is seemly for me to hold dominion over thee, for I am clever and shifty." The copper pot replied: "Well known is thy shiftiness. If thy claim is just, let us essay to proceed together, battle line facing battle line." And they journeyed as if bound together, joined at their two shoulders. The copper pot went a straight course because of its weight, but the clay pot overturned from its face to its belly because of its lightness, and showed a back side instead of a face, and it went a crooked way. The wind cast it upon the pot of copper, and the waves abetted the wind, and they cracked and shattered the clay pot on the copper.

The parable is for a poor man who strives to overreach the rich. He cannot vie with one stronger than he, and when he vaunts himself over him he is humbled and outstripped, for the race is not to the swift.

34

Frog & Oxen

WHO BOASTS OF HIS DEEDS
MUST BEWARE LEST HIS SHAME
BE REVEALED.

A FROG saw oxen in their ploughing approach the reeds and marsh of her tent and hastened forward to meet them. She inquired their name and the name of their father, for she desired their acquaintance. Said she: "Mine is wisdom and counsel to diagnose every wound or ailment and to apply bandages and potent remedies. By the aspects of the urine and the pulse of the arm I discern improvement or the reverse, and I have restored health to many; as I interpreted, so it came to pass." An elderly ox looked upon her that was boasting for her manifold wisdom and said to her: "If thy words are true, why is thy appearance as of one dead? Thou art the meagerest of all

creeping things, as if tomorrow thou wouldst descend t
the grave. But wisdom is recognized by its effects; wisdom quickeneth its owner's life. In thee there is no ruddiness, but thou art all green; before thee I cannot forbear
spitting." The frog was overwhelmed with shame and
sunk her head between her two thighs. She went speedily
to hide in her covert of reeds and fens.

The parable is for one who boasts of his wisdom and
achievements. Let him beware lest his shame be proven
upon him, for it is better to remain silent until others
speak of one's splendor than to exchange honor for disgrace. There are some whom others praise and introduce
into the presence of the great. And the sage hath said
[Proverbs 27.2]: "Let another praise thee, and not thine
own mouth."

35
Mouse & Hole

WHOSO LORDS IT OVER THE WEALTH
OF STRANGERS WILL RID HIMSELF
OF IT EVEN AS HE SWALLOWED IT.

A MOUSE lean and black entered a granary through a
hole and put his tooth to the grain. He ate and was
satisfied and grew fat; he covered his face with fatness, and
his little finger was thicker than the loins he had brought
thither in the beginning. When he wished to return upon
his path he could not pass through the hole by which he
had come. The cat looked at him and said: "The hole is
not of a size with thee. Mouse, what is this thou hast done?

Thou art waxen fat, thou art grown thick, thou art covered with fatness. Before thou return by this path the fat of thy flesh must grow lean. Never shalt thou see the fathers thou didst know if thou vomit not forth that which thou hast swallowed." The keepers of the granary heard him, and they chased him and smote him and bruised him.

The parable is for a man whose heart made him lord it over the wealth of strangers. Even as he swallowed so did he rid himself of it. A host he swallowed, but he spewed it forth; in the half of his days it forsook him.

36

Wolf & Cattle

WHOSE FEET ARE ACCUSTOMED TO
ROBBERY'S PATH, HIS EYE WILL
NOT SPARE ANOTHER'S WEALTH.

A WOLF who was the king's vizier and a chief made it
his goal to destroy all flesh. He robbed and ravaged,
plundered and uprooted; all that he found he pierced.
And the beasts and the fowl and the cattle upon whose
families confusion had been visited went to the lion to
complain of him. Said the lion: "Evil it is and rebellious
if, as ye say, he hath bared his teeth. Hath he indeed destroyed according as the cry that hath come unto me? I
shall judge him, so that he will turn his back from destroying, and I shall cast the prey from his teeth." And he
sent word to the wolf: "Come unto me on the morrow.
Hearken and obey, delay not." So he came, and the lion
addressed him with sternness and said to him: "Wherefore hast thou done so? No more crush the neck of the
cattle, nor rend the beasts for prey. Thine own food are
such carcasses and mangled bodies of fowl or cattle as
thou wilt find dead in the field. But the living thou shalt
not lurk after nor hunt down. If thou canst not keep my
words, swear to me that thou wilt not eat meat for two
full years, to atone for thy sins, which are inscribed and
sealed. This is the sentence that I determine for thee." So
the wolf swore this matter: that he would not eat flesh for
two years from the day he preyed upon any that dwelt
among the beasts. The wolf departed thence and went
upon his way, and the lion was left king in his lair. The
wolf ate not of any four-legged creature, in keeping with
the oath which he sware, unless he found some mangled

body or carcass cast out into the field or upon the road. One day when he was famished he turned this way and that and saw a fat kid, desirable to look upon and good to eat; and he said: "Who can keep the commandment?" Within him his thoughts were at war whether to set his face against the kid, and he said in his heart: "If my lust vanquish me and I again smite a living creature as I have done aforetime, from that day I must count two full years during which I must not eat flesh. This is the thing I sware to the king; but my heart hath devised a way to fulfill mine oath: The days of the year number three hundred and sixty-five; let the opening of my eyes be reckoned a day, and their closing a new night." And he opened his eyes after that he had shut them tight, and the evening and the morning were the first day. So doing he counted two years, and his iniquity was removed and his sin atoned. Then his eyes turned to the kid of their choice and looked upon him and pierced him; and he said: "Lo, I have made atonement before my food." So he seized the kid by the neck and cut it up and ate it, as was his wont in the beginning. Still is his arm stretched out against living things, as in days of old and years gone by.

The parable is for a man wont ever to steal and rob, whose eye spares not the wealth of others. Their wealth and their toil he spoils and plunders; and if he swear in the presence of all, his heart will cunningly circumvent his oath and he will account himself innocent of his curse.

37

Eagle, Fowl, Lion, Beasts, Bat

HE WHO SPEAKS SMOOTH WORDS
WILL BE FELLOW TO THE STRONG
IN OPPRESSION.

T HE EAGLE ruled over all winged creatures, whether on land or bough, and the lion over all cattle and beasts from all remote ends of the earth. The eagle and the birds made war with the lion and all the beasts and cattle. Said the bat in his heart, for wickedness engulfed him: "Verily, I have wings like the birds and feet like the cattle and beasts. I know not which host will prevail over the other, or who will die or be taken captive or be crushed. I shall stand spectator and see whether he be strong or weak, and my hand shall be with the folk whose hand prospers and prevails." So he withdrew from the host and stood over against it to see what would befall. He took his stand upon a tall tree in the distance and said: "It is a time of battle for the birds and not a time of play. I shall lift mine eyes to the victors to help them. I shall abide quiet and look forth from my mansion." When he saw that the beasts had the upper hand and that confusion had fallen upon the host of the birds, he descended from the tree and went on all fours, and swore to all the beasts and the cattle to help with all his might. And he said: "Be strong and do battle. Let not the winged creatures escape; let every man be zealous against them." But as the day waned toward evening the battle waxed strong; the birds gathered might, and confusion fell upon the lion's host. Said the bat in his heart: "I will return to mine own people; I will no longer continue in sorrow with the lion's host. I will fly up and perch, and I will hide my feet under my wings." So he gathered his feet between his shoulders to make himself wings and quickly flew among the birds and said: "Strengthen your weak hands and inflict bruises and wounds and festering sores upon the beasts and the cattle that walk on all fours." But the birds recognized the bat and said: "Why art thou so transformed to walk among us so willfully? In the morning we saw thee with the lion's host, walking on all fours like them, when their hand was strong; and thou didst put thy hand forth against our position, when thou wert a bird like ourselves. But when we prevailed, then didst thou spread thy wings toward us. Blood hast thou hated, and blood will pursue thee. Wherefore hast thou mocked thy skin and worked deception and unrighteousness? Thy ambush is within thee, for now that thou art returned to those of whom thou wert ashamed, the iniquity in thee is found out. This shall be thy penalty: Thou shalt be accounted among the species of creeping things. A wanderer and a vagabond shalt thou be in the land. For that thou hast played the stranger with thy fellows so shall thy seed be, black and plucked and bald and blind, and strangers in our midst. Thou shalt no more walk with neck outstretched. The light of the sun will be for thee blindness. Leprous and a vermin shalt thou be called. Of every encounter shalt thou be afraid." So they conspired against him, and they brought him to the eagle, who said: "Is this he who simulated the cattle and the beasts? For that his spirit is lying he shall be plucked and bald and shall flee from the light of the sun. In the evening he shall flit about as one confused. Not even in the tenth generation shall he enter into the congregation. He shall not avail to stand upon his feet if the sun shine upon him." And so they plucked him and scraped him and blinded his eyes, and they drove him confounded from the dwelling places which they inhabited, and all the birds of heaven became strangers unto him. Now he is like neither bird nor beast; they call him vermin upon the earth.

The parable is for one who sees his friend or relative fall under the power of his enemy, and addresses the enemy with blandishing words. With the strong he pretends strength, for crooked gain; but if the lowly acquire firmness and strength, with his false heart he returns to become his comrade, for he knows no shame or remorse. And with this comradeship he acts deceitfully, saying: "Lo, I have strengthened and helped thee and with the right hand of my righteousness I supported thee when the hand of thine enemy was strong upon thee. I did not slacken in the day of tribulation." What befell the bat will befall him in the end, and he will leave no name or remnant. His fate is fitted to the pattern carved: The wicked shall not be unpunished.

38

Hare & Hounds

HE WHOM FORTUNE GOVERNS
SHALL NOT SPEEDILY FIND ESCAPE.

A HARE and her children resolved to leave the place where they dwelt, for they found no respite there. The dogs were harsh of soul and always pursued after them; they ran and never tired, they walked and grew not weary. Said the hares: "Lo, we are left few out of many, and the fire that rages against us is never quenched. Even in our chambers there is dread, and our spirit can no longer stand erect. Let us journey forth and go to a field where there is none to track and chase us." One of the family, upon whom rested the spirit of wisdom, made answer: "If ye will accede to my counsel and hearken to the instruction of my lips, ye will not remove hence.

Many have I seen journey from their place and their native land, but they have returned to the spot of their shame; where they had hoped to find a land peaceful and serene, they found twofold perturbation. For living creatures have no governance over their lot to escape the machinations of fate. He that acknowledges his own abiding place will not change or seek a substitute for it; for wherever the soles of your feet tread, the voice of terror will be in your ears." But they hearkened not to what he had said to them and forsook their place and their tents. They walked until the sun set and there was no light; and all, great and small, encamped by the bank of a river. But when they thought to find a resting place for the soles of their feet, lo, frogs' voices roared from the river, and dread and terror fell upon all the hares; one lamented bitterly with his voice, and one scurried from his place, one went a crooked way. There was no refuge for the swift of foot. When dawn broke, lo, there were men passing and returning upon the road, riding upon horses, with dogs before them. Their yelping was loud as they sniffed from the road the tracks of the hares scattered over the field, and the riders tarred them on to spread confusion among them, and they smote them and desolated them. The remnant said: "We will return to our people and our native place. Alas for the day that our souls were impatient of hearing the counsel of the sage and our hearts were enticed to folly! Better for us was it then than now." So with souls grieving and sorrowing the remnant that survived turned back until they came to the land of their dwelling.

The parable is for a man whom fortune governs. He says: "I will make my wandering far, I will seek me a refuge"; and he forsakes his place and his native land. But his glory shall not abide upon the path which he takes. If one say to him: "Cast thy desires upon thy creator and endure his destiny; who can straighten that which he hath made crooked? Abide until the storm shall pass from thy tent and the spirit of the ruler favor thee"—he will not hearken nor consent. The many who heed not counsel are as fickle as coracles; they journey forth from the tents which they had fixed fast. Better than fine gold and than jasper set and enclosed in a ring, is when the wise admonishes an ear that hearkens.

39

Starling, Eagle, Birds

THE SMALL MAY HOPE
FOR LORDSHIP, FOR WISDOM
IS BETTER THAN STRENGTH.

A STARLING came to rule by reason of his wisdom and not his great strength; though he was smaller than all winged creatures, he was raised and exalted over them. When the birds foregathered in the beginning and took counsel to set as king over them what bird would soar highest in their camp, the eagle said: "Who among those that fly is as I am, and who but me is swift?" When the starling heard this, he plotted in his thoughts to make his perch firm on the eagle's wing; wherever the eagle would fly, there would his own encampment be; the eagle would bear him upon his pinions. So he hid on the eagle's wing, as he had planned; and when all the winged creatures soared, the eagle rose twice as high into heaven as any bird that flew, and he said: "I am king over all the birds, for I have enlarged and exalted myself." While he was yet speaking, the starling came; he had hidden under his wing and until then had rested on his back, so that his reason stood firm within him. When he saw that the eagle was weary and his hands were lax, he gathered his strength and girded himself to fly higher, above the eagle. So they gave him the majesty of kingship and royalty.

The parable is for a man filled with silver and gold, beneath whom the supporters of pride are humble, while he boasts of his painted chambers. But the strong must not glory in his strength to despise the humble and the small; for time will turn to be his pursuer and will cast him down from his ambitions, and a humble man with understanding will search him out. Right is the saying of the sage to make wise: "Better is wisdom than strength."

40

Bear & Doe

LET A MAN'S SOUL NOT BE
PRECIOUS IN HIS EYES, TO ESCAPE
IN PLACE OF HIS SONS.

A BEAR saw a pregnant doe whose labors had seized her so that she travailed sore. The bear perceived that her time was come to give birth and that her bearing was difficult, and in his cunning said to her: "Hasten, dispatch thy throes, for I shall put mine eye upon thee for kindness and upon the fawns thou wilt bear, if I know where they are. Leave thy sons; I will give them life and find their sufficiency of food. There shall be a covenant of peace between me and thee forever." It was in slyness that the bear spoke, to devour her young; but she made her reply with wisdom: "I know thine eyeballs look fairly upon me in the innocence of thy heart and the purity of thy hands, and I rejoice in thy saying. Thou hast spread thy wings over thy handmaiden. But I beseech you, my lord, fulfill my request: Remove thee two bowshots from upon me, for in the article of birth it brings us shame if males look upon us. Pass over from me, and thou shalt be the diligent one who profiteth. Look not behind thee and stand not in all the plain. This day it is not proper for males to be with females in their environs. I can do nothing until thou go hence. Already had I given birth, hadst thou not restrained me for my great shame." So the bear went and sat afar, the distance of two bowshots; and when she saw that he was far off, the doe's feet carried her away. By her wariness she delivered her own life and the life of her sons.

The parable is that a man should not hold his own soul precious, to escape from the snares of death, and give his son in his place. A woman big of belly should not make her life precious in her eyes, saying: "Would I might empty my full belly, for until now have I labored for vanity." Like the doe she should take her life in her hands to deliver her offspring by flattery and deception.

41

Peacock, Wheat, Crane

A MAN'S PRIDE WILL BRING HIM
LOW, AND HE SHALL NOT AVAIL
TO ENTER INTO JUDGMENT
WITH ONE STOUTER THAN HE.

THE COLORFUL bird called peacock found a heap of wheat, and the crane also came and set his mouth to the grain. Said the peacock to the crane: "Why hast thou no awe of me? Who art thou to associate with me? What hath chaff to do with corn? Who is so beautiful as I among all the fowl, and to whom wilt thou liken me to be mine equal? Who can find any taint in me? My plumage is as a coat of many colors, and princes and princesses make headdresses of my tail to wear as tiaras. Have I peers? Who can recount my splendor? Happy the fowl to whom I communicate my secrets. Gold exceeding fine is the crown of my head. Mine is glory and dominion. No bird is like me for beauty. Mine is the plumage and mine the broidery. My tail is beyond calculation; two cubits and a half is its length. But thou art like a thief, curtailed for his crime. Why art not in fear and dread to enter into the same camp with me? Depart, and let us be two camps. Thy meagerness cannot be described." Answered the crane: "If my twigs are silent, yet thy lies make men hold their peace. Why dost thou vaunt thy tail and feathers? Let another praise thee, and not thine own mouth; a stranger, and not thine own lips. If thou art comely in thine own eyes, thou art lowly and feeble for thy size, lowly in voice and lowly in stature. Thou walkest not forth with a high hand and art undone by the rebuke of any fowl. Thou canst not fly like them, and therefore thou dwellest on dry land. But lo, my sheaf arose and also stood upright; my neck is long, my throat outstretched. I make my shout heard among the stars. My legs are straight; of me was it said, Thy stature is like to a palm tree. It is not out of weakness but out of strength that my tail is short; to cast dread upon mine enemies I gird my loins for battle. But thine ornateness is only a flaw. Favor is deceitful and beauty is vain." When the peacock heard this stern speech he fell mute, for it was time to be silent.

The parable is for one who boasts of his beauty. If his heart is empty of wisdom, this is his flaw; for a man's pride will bring him low, and he cannot enter into judgment with one stouter than he. Pleasant indeed is the saying of the Arab sage: "A man can bequeath his son nothing better than wisdom." He that boasts of beauty and wealth is smitten with blindness, for what avails an open eye if the heart is unseeing?

42

Smith & Bramblebush

AMONG ALL MEN ON THE FACE
OF THE DRY LAND THERE ARE MANY
WHO REPAY EVIL FOR GOOD.

A N IRONSMITH labored and toiled and with his strong arm fashioned a peerless axe of steel. Its edge he whetted to remove its bluntness. Then he inquired of his neighbors whence he might procure suitable wood, for he desired to make a strong helve and sought timber that would not rot. His advisers responded as follows: "Take thee of the branch of the bramblebush; it is tougher than all other wood and will last forever." So he went to the bramblebush according to this counsel and cut a branch. Laboriously he fitted the wood he prepared to the steel, and fashioned the axe and finished it, saying of the joint, "It is good." To make trial of its goodness and beauty he seized the axe and cut the bramblebush down entirely, root and branch, for its day was come.

The parable is for a man who loved his neighbor and cosseted him and made much of him, and fed him and gave him drink when he was hungry and naked and needy. But when he saw him waxed fat and grown great he turned wicked and betrayed the kindness he had done him, and requited him evil instead of good and enmity instead of love. And he hated him with bitter hatred, more than any man on earth. Their nobles shall be of themselves, and their governor shall proceed from the midst of them. Shall the axe boast itself against him that heweth therewith? What this man finds is bitterer than death; his destroyers and they that make him waste shall go forth out of himself.

43

Wolf, Dog, Flock

A MAN MUST NOT BETRAY HIS FAITH
NOR VIOLATE HIS COMMANDMENT.

A WOLF who was in fear of a dog carried a loaf of bread to the sheep which were enclosed within a hedge. The dog awoke from his sleep, and the wolf in his cunning said to him: "Know that what is mine is thine. Take my blessing which I have brought thee; but not by bread alone will I be thy helpmeet. Take all I have that is desirable, but for the present, eat bread." The dog answered: "In vain hast thou wearied thy footsteps; though thou urge me I shall not eat thy bread, for it is the bread of falsehood. In my sight thy words are not good; not for my benefit hast thou brought me bread from thy house, but to stop my mouth lest I raise my voice against thee when thou spoilest the sheep. Thou didst think to find a favorable opportunity; but far be it from me to quench the candle of my honor. My master has entrusted the sheep to my hand; how shall I betray my faith? I love my master and my house; from my youth he has brought me up, as a father. But for thy cajoling words thou shalt grieve." The dog whetted his tongue against him, and the shepherd arose in anger and ran with the dog to chase away the wolf, who hated him in his heart.

The parable is for a man who guards his spirit lest he prove faithless and make his way crooked. In his mouth and in his heart the law is one. For no reward or bribe will he betray his faith nor will he cheat his comrade to raise his heel against him. Not from granary or winepress but from the dog he draweth his example, for he is not corrupted by bribery. And the sage hath said: "Cleave unto faith and keep the commandment, for no wealth is greater than forsaking lust."

44

Kite & Doves

HE THAT BESTOWETH HONOR UPON
HIS DESTROYER ACQUIRETH
A MASTER OVER HIMSELF.

A KITE dwelt and watched among the doves, and if one
was alone he flew with him and would suddenly
strike and devour him; in the flicker of an eye he disap-
peared. The doves consulted amongst themselves, for the
kite deceived them, and resolved to seek his peace and to
conclude a covenant with him if he would walk in innocence and uprightness with them. They said to him: "Thou
shalt be our lord; come thou and rule over us, and our
weak hands shall be strengthened, for the birds will fear
thee." So they gave him dominion and the majesty of
royalty, and he was received into their company. But each
day the kingship afflicted them with wrath outpoured, for
he robbed them and their company, and tore and plucked
their plumage. He said to them: "How can ye stand in the
place of my coming? If I am lord where is my terror?"
And he preyed upon them and devoured them in every
corner, and none stirred his wing nor opened his mouth to
chirp, and they that remained fled to the hills. They were
wearied and sickened of their lives, and confusion fell upon their families. The doves of the valleys all murmured
and said: "What is this we have done to put over us a
brazen-faced king? What he hath formerly done in secret
he now doth in the open. Who shall be left? Better our
life without him, when we could take pleasant counsel
with him."

The parable is for a man who gives honor to one who

is his destroyer; he acquires a master over himself. Better that his eyes should avoid him than that he should speak with him, good or evil. For he nurseth rebellion in his heart, and ever is his ambush within him. The man who serves and honors him will rejoice and be glad at his doom. And the sage hath said: "Honor him thou lovest and he will love thee; beware of him thy heart hateth."

45
Cormorant & Birds

A MAN FILLED WITH VIOLENCE
SHALL BE FOR A SPOIL IN THE
LAND OF HIS HABITATION.

Among the birds the cormorant was for a scorn and a reproach, for his was the shame of the backside. Through the aperture he ejected his excrements a thousand times in an instant; his stench was noisome at all times and he made their camp unclean. They hated him sore and banished him from their world, saying: "Without the camp shall be thy resting place, and thou shalt turn and cover thine excrements. The plague of emerods is in thee, and it seals thy passages; our doom for thee is death." He stood rooted in shame, for he was a mockery and a laughing stock. And he saw a place afar off, atop a lofty hill, and there he sat with soul downcast. But even there he found no rest, for the winged creatures sent a messenger to bid him depart. And he said: "I stand in awe of every bird in the land of my habitation. I will fly away and settle at the end of the sea; I will wander far off to a distant country. No longer will I hear the voice of oppressors and persecutors, and there shall I be honored instead of being despised and lightly esteemed. There is none that holdeth with me in this matter." So he flew toward the sea. At eventide the raven encountered him and said: "Whither goest, cormorant? Surely thou seekest a resting place which shall please thee?" And he answered: "I shall find me a resting place beyond the sea, for thy fellows have driven me from my heritage and cried 'Unclean, unclean!' against me." Said the raven: "Carriest thou with thee thy rear, which hath driven thee far from thy resting place?" The cormorant answered: "My rear I cannot leave behind me, for I have carried that shame from my youth." Said the raven: "That will be a scorn and a mockery to thee wheresoever thy foot treads. Just as thy friends have turned into enemies because of it here, so there all that go and come will keep far from thee. Abundant plumage and mighty limbs will not avail thee, for thou wilt be helpless and crushed."

The parable is of a violent man who is for a spoil in the land of his habitation for that he treads the bow of his tongue for falsehood, is a talebearer, a betrayer of secrets, and a searcher for gossip to which he may add falsehood. When he sees that his fellows hate him he journeys far from his dwelling place, where he has wrought no good among his people but put forth his hand against men who wished him well; but there they hate him as men had done in his former place. Death and life are in the power of the tongue. Of the bearers of slander our sages have said: "This shall be the law of the leprous." And the Arab hath said: "Ere thou utterest thy word consider what its end will be." For as a man undergoes cautery to remedy his body, so should he labor to heal his soul of the incidence of flattery and cruelty and to remove his destroyer from his tongue.

46

Cat & Mouse

THERE IS DELIVERY AND RECOURSE
FOR AN OATH TAKEN UNDER DURESS.

A CAT went forth one morning to hunt his food, and he
saw over against him a mouse in a vessel full of
strong drink; this had befallen him because he could not
make his way out. The cat, hungry and eager, went toward him joyfully. There he would display the inveterate
hatred which was his guilt, for he hated the mouse from
yesterday and the day before. He sprang to the lip of the
vessel and crouched and rose against him and lifted his
voice against the mouse and framed false charges against
him, saying: "My righteousness and thy guilt have driven
thee thither. Woe to them that rise early in the morning
to pursue strong drink! Hasten, come forth, stand not; I
shall work my will upon thee. Thy sorrow shall be turned
to my delight, for thy flesh is dainty." The mouse made
answer: "I am oppressed and tormented, I am plucked
and bald, without taste or flavor. I have fallen and cannot
rise, I am broken down and cut off. The fat of my flesh
hath grown lean from the day I fell into this pit, and my
countenance testifieth to my sore grief and affliction. Now
for a month nor bread nor pottage hath passed my lips. If
gladness hath burgeoned within thee, rejoice not when
thine enemy is fallen. Work no ill against me now, deliver me that I sink not, and I will make thee my bene-
ficiary. At the appointed time I shall return to thee, and I
shall be plump and my hair sprouted; when I return thou
shalt rejoice in my flesh. Only bring my soul forth from
its straits, for the waters have risen over my head." He
raised his hand to the cat that he would return to him at

the appointed time and show himself in a month. And he swore an oath: If the cat would deliver him from captivity, he would keep his covenant and stand fast by it. So the cat who was his troubler turned to be his helper; he remembered not his hatred but drew the mouse out of the strong drink. But when the mouse was departed from the cat he turned his back and rebelled against him. He feasted his heart with all good things and tarried beyond the appointed term. The cat sent him word, saying: "Thy covenant thou must keep; thou must return to my domain, plump and fat as thou hast sworn. Let not thy footsteps tarry, for thou hast added to thy term. If thou deceive me and abide, then give thy son in thy stead." The mouse acknowledged his oath, but declared that it was given under duress, for he was confronted with ruin when he swore. Furthermore, it was in drunkenness that he had recklessly sworn, when he was not master of himself. The oath was given both in drunkenness and under coercion; law is for life, not death. With such a claim he escaped, and the cat had no power over him.

The parable is for a dispute between two men, where each studies and seeks to transform the complaint to a plot or accident, to be acquitted of offense, for what is done under duress or in drunkenness has no validity but is accounted youthful folly. And the sage hath said to his son [Ecclesiastes 10.2]: "A wise man's heart is at his right side." If thou art wise thou wilt be enlarged and exalted. Be not wise in words if thou art not so in deed, for when a man's words do not resemble his deeds, it is folly on his part and shame.

47

Ass in Lion's Skin

IF THE SPIRIT OF PRIDE HATH
BREATHED IN A MAN, THE SPIRIT
OF WISDOM IS NOT IN HIM.

An ass went from his master's house to graze in the hills and high places, and there he found the flayed skin of a lion. In this he resolved to clothe himself, and he put his hands forth to throw it over him before and behind and over the smooth of his neck and his hands. His heart was uplifted and he walked in pride, exalting himself and saying: "I shall be king." And he went to terrorize the beasts in the hills and the valleys, and like a lion he hunted and tracked man and beast in the fields. For fear of him the shepherds abandoned the keeping of their sheep, for they thought he was a lion, when he was only an ass; and the tillers of soil fled before him nor pastured their sheep and kine. Each cried to his brother: "Hear thou me; cast away the sheep which is thy wealth, for he that shall be found in the field shall not live." To them the ass was a lion; and out of his heart's delight at being thought a lion he dealt frowardly with his master and said: "He shall no longer lay burdens upon me." The ass knew not his master's crib and returned not to his house; but he cast his terror over all that walked on fours, for so had he vehemently sworn in his pride. A report was heard: "A lion hath gone up from his lair. Gird ye every man his sword upon his thigh and we shall surround him with spears and snares; mayhap we shall avail to smite him. If we trap him in forest or plain we shall send him to the king for a gift." The master of the ass said to his neighbors: "I have lost my ass, but how shall I seek him?—The lion may make me his prey." One day the master went and wrapped his face in his mantle, and came to one of the hills. There he saw his ass disguised as a lion to terrify all that caught sight of him. By his stature and tail and ears the master recognized his ass, and when he saw his master the ass cast his eyes down. Said the master: "Because thy heart was high and thine ambush within thee, because thou hast made bold to shed innocent blood and cast thy terror in the land of the living, hast walked with neck out-stretched, hast dreamed and thyself interpreted, hast been enticed by the rebelliousness of thy heart to become stranger to thy master and thy tasks, thy toil and thy yoke shall be made heavy and thou shalt be cast down to the dust. Thou shalt not pursue the sheep as if they were thy booty. Now remove thine adornment, and I will make thee stand naked as on the day of thy birth; thy glory will turn to thy doom. Thou shalt know who thou art and whence thou comest, and whether thou hast seen thy father king over the beasts." The ass was stripped of his adornment, and received twofold punishment from his master for his rebelliousness.

The parable is for a vile and nameless man over whom a breeze wafts so that he sins and the spirit of pride stirs in him; there is no spirit of wisdom within him. A people who knew him not serve him, and they honor him in his walking and his sitting down, for in his walking abroad he is recognized only by his garb and his fine raiment. He deals haughtily with them, saying, "I have found them slaves." His crest was among thick boughs, and he walked with neck outstretched, forgetting who his fathers were. He vaunted his height and the length of his branches, but when they recognized his taint and the taint of his fathers they exchanged his glory for shame.

And I plied my poesy and said:

An ass clothed himself in lion's skin he found,

And his approach frightened bear and leopard.
So the vile one who clothes him in fine linen and is
   proud,
But knows not decently to lift head or feet.

48

Fox & Crane

TO MAKE THE PATH OF HIS DEEDS
STRAIGHT A MAN SHOULD
COMPANY WITH HIS EQUAL.

THE FOX said to the crane: "Why art thou ever shut in? Come and dine with me, and see my house and my people." And he enticed him to come with him, to be merry with him and eat his bread. The fox dashed forward for flesh; he made a sudden attack upon the poultry and smote a hen who had closed her eyeballs in the face of the sun and had sighed and spread her wings. While the fox prepared his repast he devised cunning plots and said in his heart: "Lo, simple am I if I do not eat of what I have prepared and only lick the food which is so sweet, while the crane swallows the whole at once." With his wonted slyness he ground his food fine and spread it upon the table and invited the crane to eat. But the crane could take none into his mouth, for it was not his manner to eat food fine and scattered and spread. But the eye of the fox took no pity upon him, and he left the table empty, even as the ox licketh up the grass of the field. But the crane returned to his house fordone and weary, hungry and heavy and depressed. He spoke not to the fox, neither showing his impatience nor concealing it, but in his reins he was perplexed and sought to exact vengeance. While he was devising a plan, a tree taught him his invention: All its limbs were full of apertures, and these holes he filled with provision. Any food he prepared he thrust into the hole, so deep that none could find it, and it would be his with no stranger to share. The crane bored a hole in his door whereby he entered his domain, and there deposited his food. Then he invited the fox and urged him to come

with him; and he showed him the food and said: "What is before thee is thine; eat as is good in thy sight." But the fox could not lick it free with his tongue to subject it to his tooth; neither with tongue nor paw could he move it. At this the crane rejoiced, for he could bring the food out and eat it heartily in the presence of the fox. He requited the fox for his deed; as he did, so was it done to him.

The parable is for one who seeks plots and accidents and contrivances to befool his neighbor that is a perfect and upright man and dwells with him in security. The other will become infected by his composition and his malefactions, in the way that he has taught. The stouthearted are spoiled and their heart is as fat as grease. He thinks to find good when he doeth ill. How can he harvest wheat who sows thorns? He that fashions calamity for his neighbor, the instrument of his wounding is in his own hand.

49

Sow, Doe, Beasts

IF A MAN'S SOUL IS POLLUTED AND DEFILED
HE CANNOT EASILY BE HEALED.

A sow of the forest wallowed in the mire and found delight in trampling the muck. In the forest there was the sound of banqueting and gaiety, of a board laden with dainties, for the stag was marrying his kinswoman, and all that walked on fours had assembled at his wedding canopy. Each feasted and was filled with bread and meal, flesh and fish, all eating and making merry in their gladness; great and small participated in the festivities for seven days. The sow heard the sound of rejoicing but laid it not upon her heart. A deer looked upon the sow, her gaping mouth befouled with filth for she had rooted in the dung heap, had eaten to her full, and showed the remains, and the deer said to the sow: "Come to the house of the bride, where is the sound of a happy throng. Thou shalt lack nothing; all that thine eyes ask, thou shalt there take; not by measure shalt thou there eat thy bread. Present there is every bird after its kind. His ornament maketh the stag master, and the spirit of joy prevails mightily in his heart. The winged creatures utter song. There are viands of all manner in abundance, and vessels of diverse sorts. The amiable doe hath made herself beautiful for the stag, and over all the canopy is a glorious shelter." Answered the sow: "If indeed food of all sorts was there, did ye eat bran steeped in hot water and mire trampled in the streets? There is no dainty like them in all the land, and if these two are withheld then all the rest is nothing worth in my sight, for from the day of my birth I have tasted no viands as delightful as these."

The parable is for one whose comportment is repulsive and whose lust never abandons the glitter of his sins, until his soul is defiled and polluted. The healing of his transgressions is negligible, for his errors flourish within him and he does deeds which are not done. His heart hath played the harlot by the path of his eyes; and even when he grows old, he will never depart from his ways. In the eyes of his neighbors he is abominable and filthy, for he hath troubled the waters with his feet. When his comrades say: "Lo, how goodly and how pleasant it is to cleave to the way of the upright and innocent, whose portion is for life and for whom much good is stored up; be thou strong and do as they do."—Then will he say: "That which I have tried I love, for I have made lying my shelter and by falsehood am I hidden. I will fulfill my desire and satisfy my lust to add drunkenness to thirst. Better for me is the pleasure of my eyes and the enjoyment of my inclinations than to await royalty in another world. I shall have peace, for I shall walk in the imagination of my heart."

50

Lion, Beasts, Ape

MASTER AND CONSTRAIN THY
HEART TO BRING ALL THINGS
NEAR AND KEEP THEM NOT AFAR.

THE LION published a notice throughout his realm that all that walked on fours should attend him on an appointed day. He wished to know which was superior in favor and comeliness, beautiful of form and beautiful of aspect, for he intended to make that one who won favor in the eyes of his beholders second to himself in authority. When they were all gathered together, the ape said: "None bears such favor as my son or is so handsome and so adorned. How great is his goodness, and how great his beauty! The majesty of my lord the king will be increased and augmented by my son, he will find thine own pleasure and speak thy words."

They that speak in parables say: To him that loveth toad and mouse they appear as two great lights. Therefore should every man compel and constrain his heart to bring his neighbor near and not keep him afar. Even if the fire of hatred burns in him like a flame, his left hand should repel but his right hand bring near.

51

Four Oxen & a Lion

A COMPANY FREE OF TERROR IS
THE DWELLING OF BRETHREN TOGETHER.

FOUR OXEN agreed to unite into a fellowship, bound close together and not separated. They concluded a covenant and were moved by a single spirit. Many days they continued in this fellowship; when they stood they stood together and when they walked they walked together. A lion circled about the four of them but saw that their time was not come, for they stood as one in the battlefield, and because they were four, they were stout in their going forth. The lion brooded in his soul, month by month, how he could bring destruction upon them if their bond were loosed. One day he stood from afar and gaped his maw wide for he was hungry and weary; hope long deferred had made him heavy and displeased. He called to the ox whose feet stood in the plain and cajoled him by the smoothness of his lips until he separated him from his band; and when he was separated from his fellows, the lion dedicated him to evil, for he spoiled him in his anger and devoured him. The voice of the three that were left in the camp terrified him not, nor did he make answer to their bellowing.

The parable: How goodly and how pleasant it is when the counsel of comrades is gathered together in sweetness. When brethren dwell together, their fellowship is free of fear. Their enticers are as waters that fail. They consult only to cast down and their goal is guile, to separate their victims from their fellowship and alienate them from their delight. With him who has strayed from the band the treacherous dealer dealeth treacherously and the spoiler spoileth. The wise take it not to heart if their associate is slandered; they have ears but hear not, for their soul is pure and innocent and they abhor the false tongue of them that work deception. The bond between two wise men will not be loosed, and the threefold cord is not quickly broken.

52

Lion, Wolf, Fox, Ox, Calf

THERE IS ONE WHO IS DESTROYED
WITHOUT JUDGMENT, BUT THE TONGUE
OF THE WISE IS FOR A HEALING.

A LION who ruled by his strength summoned a wolf and a fox to his presence and said to them: "A month past my lioness bore me a cub; let us go together and bring provision for her." So the two went with him. Their king passed before them, and their hearts were fortified with gladness at his fellowship. The three strode boldly on. In the field they looked about them like spoilers, and upon that day they broke the necks of an ox, a cow, and a calf. Said the lion to the fox: "Thou hast been set on high; is thy heart within thee uncircumcised that thou knowest not how to divide booty without lots?" The fox answered and said: "I am young in years, whereas the wolf is reckoned amongst the exceeding wise, and the passage of years implants knowledge. His apportionment will be perfect." The lion said to the wolf: "Why is the wise loath to choose portions? All that issueth from his mouth shall stand fast." The wolf answered: "The ox is for my lord the lion, and the cow shall be brought to his mate, the lioness; the calf shall be divided between me and the fox." Said the lion: "In rebelliousness and treachery and guilt and frowardness and intransigence thou hast not remembered a portion for my firstborn son. Therefore thy blood is upon thy head, and I shall make thy soul grieve." He drew his hand upon him and smote him and flayed him of his skin head to foot until his skull and hide wallowed in blood. He said to the fox: "At thy word shall the booty be divided." And the fox answered: "I shall divide it with justice and equity. To my lord the king, the ox; to the lioness, the cow. For the cub in whom thy heart rejoiceth I adjudge the calf as a portion." Said the lion: "There is none so wise and understanding as thou in all my realm. From this day forward I shall make thee my confidant, for in mine eyes thou art very desirable. From whom hast thou learnt to divide booty?" The fox answered: "When I saw the miter upon the wolf's head wrapped in blood when he stumbled in the utterance of his lips, and that a deceived heart led him astray—therefore did I not allow my tongue to sin."

The parable: A man must not hasten to speak before one that is stronger than he. He shall fashion a bridle for his spirit and acquire counsel, that he make not his path crooked, for some are destroyed without judgment. But the tongue of the wise is for a healing; for he reflects and ponders, but delays the words of his mouth. The wise man is instructed by the example of another. And the sage hath said in his book of instruction [Proverbs 19.25]: "Smite a scorner, and the simple will beware." And the Arab in his wisdom hath said: "The portion of one man is from his ear to his soul, and the portion of one man from his tongue to another."

53

Sun, Wind, Man

THE WISE MAN ACHIEVES MORE
BY HIS WISDOM THAN THE STRONG
BY HIS STRENGTH.

SUN AND WIND compared their qualities. Said the sun
to the wind: "I am upright and innocent, and for my
great beauty they have made me ruler over the day. If thou
boast against me, it will be accounted folly in thee, for
mine is the strength and the favor and the splendor, like
unto heaven's self for purity." Answered the wind: "If
thy merits were twice thy praise, the prevailing wind
would be thy superior. At night thou art no longer seen;
the sun knoweth his setting. But my dominion is by day
and by night; therefore it beseems me to rule. My deeds
are known in the land: I rend the mountains and break in
pieces the rocks." Said the sun: "Let us try our strength.
Here is a man coming forth toward us, clothed in tunic
and mantle. Go thou now and fight with him and wage
cunning war against him until thou strip mantle from
tunic. If he leave his garment by thy side I shall bestow the
majesty of kingship upon thee. Thy work will prosper
and thou wilt strip him: thou hast a garment: be thou
lord over us." The wind said in his heart: "I will sway
him by my cunning or strip him by my strength." So the
wind went forth in the sight of the sun and blew strong
before him. The man walked straight upon his way; when
the cold wind came out of the north, he wrapped his
mantle and tunic together and swathed himself in them so
that the wind should not come between. When the wind
put forth all the strength of his might, the man tied the
loops of his mantle around his forehead and with his right

hand grasped his skirts and made them a turban about his head; the wind did not lay bare the face of his raiment. When it appeared that the wind was wearied, for all his boasting and did not avail to wrest the mantle away and his hopes were disappointed, the sun said: "Now shalt thou see what I shall do to him." He rent his robe of darkness and his shade and dispersed all the shadows. The sun went forth over the land and confronted the man in his might; as the sun issued forth in his strength he looked upon the man from on high. When the south wind quieted the earth and the steady eye of the sun gazed upon him it wrested the weight of his garments from upon him and stripped him of his mantle. Naked did he flee that day, and availed not to carry his gear with him. When the sun shone upon him it stripped him in quietness when it reached him; not so the wind, which stormed mightily and raged.

The parable is that a wise man can achieve by his wisdom what the strong cannot by his strength. The words of the wise are as arrows in the hands of warriors and as flames of fire in a blaze. The auxiliaries of pride stoop when the gates of wisdom are opened in the wall of understanding. Though they be like gins and snares to captivate hearts, they are heard in calm; but no man has awe of a boastful fool.

54

Cedar & Bush

LET NO MAN BOAST OF HIS
WEALTH, FOR NOT FOREVER
WILL HIS LIGHT SHINE BRIGHT.

THE CEDAR of Lebanon, whose name shall be continued as long as the sun, was proud of his limbs and
his stateliness, of his height and his many branches. There
was none like him in the forest; the cedars would not hide
him. He looked about him in the camp and lo! near him
was a bush, and he said: "What hast thou to do here that
thou hast come into my boundary? How wert thou not
afraid to dwell in my shadow? Can timber be taken from
thee to do any work? Me kingship beseemeth, for I bring
forth fruit and bear branches and in me dwell winged
creatures. My little finger is thicker than thy loins. With
whom hast thou left thy briars and brambles? Thou art
only a shoot of pine, but of me they make oars and masts,
which stand as an ensign for the nations. Thy root is the
root of the broom." Answered the bush: "With the
words of thy mouth thou hast stumbled, in that thou
hast sought to boast of thy beauty. Remember that thy
place will be ploughed as a field, and they will destroy thy
stock to the root. Thine adornment of lush branches they
will cut for planks and pillars and bars. I shall look upon
thy place, and it is gone; but against us none that hews
down shall arise. Thy stateliness is turned upon thee for
destruction, to hew thy wood and cast down thy leafage.
Thy fruits every passerby will pluck and gather, while I
shall rest secure and tranquil."

The parable forbids a man to boast of beauty or riches

over his neighbor or brother or stranger. For the young lions who lack and suffer hunger will seek him day by day and he will not avail to hide; all of his days he will eat in darkness. But for the humble, over whom he has spoken strong and proud words, there may be a hope.

And I plied my poesy:

> With head bowed and heart crushed and eye lowly
> Thy steps will stand steadfast.
> See how the fire that rises is quenched in the end,
> While water that descends abides.

55
Small Fish in Net

CAST NOT AWAY WHAT IS IN THY
HAND, TO TAKE IN THY NET
WHAT IS NOT THINE.

A SMALL FISH caught in a net said to the fisherman: "I am too little to be game, that thou put me on thy hook. Spare me, that I comfort myself; thy heart will easily abandon me. Neither boiled nor roasted on the fire can I restore thy soul. Let me go and refresh myself, and I will serve thee two full years. Then wilt thou find me in my river as aforetime, large of stature and seven times as fat. If then I be boiled in water, it shall be as a festival in thy house, and then can thy heart be sustained with me." Answered the fisherman: "Better is a little fish which is now within my grasp than a great leviathan which my neighbors will rule a year hence."

The parable is known in every city, and its interpretation is familiar upon the lips of every creature: Better is a handful of satisfaction in thine own palms than heaping handfuls of hope in the hands of another. Better is a bird enclosed in a cage than two hopping on the hedge. Take what is good, even if it be little; lay your hand upon it and grasp it and let it not go. Do not choose hope deferred for doubtful increase of advantage and blessing.

56

Lion & Hunter

MANY ARE THE WORKERS OF INIQUITY
AND THE SPEAKERS OF DESTRUCTION,
FOR HEARTS ARE NOT EQUABLE.

A LION roared from within the wilderness, for he knew that a hunter of the fields was gathering his strength against him and would come thither with bow and arrows to stand stalwart against him in battle. The heart of the lion was apprehensive with fear lest the children of the man's quiver should reach his vital parts; but the hunter was twice as fearful of the lion. At length they entered sweet counsel together. With yearning eye the lion called to the man: "Keep thee, be secure, fear not, let not dread of me confound thee, for my heart longeth for thy fellowship." In purity of heart the hunter answered: "Neither shall I put my hand forth against thee." So the two walked together, with the sweetness of fellowship between them. Said the man: "I have seen all the beasts of every flesh, and I find the majesty of kingship only in one created in my form and image. In an image handsome and desirable and pleasant walketh man; therefore is his greatness increased over all the earth and he rules over all creation, even over the majestic and mighty lion in his prime." Answered the lion: "Nay, to me beseemeth kingship over all the inhabitants of earth and its isles, for I have cast my dread over all the land of the living. There is none to compare with me on earth's sands; who can stand before the roar of my voice? If I look upon him with the eye of hatred, his hopes are frustrated. Upon my neck lodges strength, and grief is rampant in the expression of my face." So they walked through all the desert, speaking their rivalry as they walked, each exalting himself over the other and saying: "I shall be king." At length they saw a heap of stones with a carved monument at their side. Graven upon the stone were a lion and a man; the man was seated on a royal throne like a king, and the lion was pictured crouching upon the soles of his feet. Said the man: "Where is thy mouth now? Shall the saw magnify itself against him that shaketh it? Now shalt thou see whether my words find their mark in thee; thou wilt find that man hath ruled over the lion from the day beasts and cattle were created, in days of old, in former years. This heap be witness and this pillar be witness; lo, my sheaf arose and also stood upright." Answered the lion: "Lo, the witness is false; if I had essayed to draw the likeness at the time appointed, I would have done to man as he devised to do to the lion; if I had desired mine own dignity the lion would be transformed to be king, with the man kneeling prostrate at his feet."

The parable: There is a man who eagerly desires to fill his soul; he looks upon all that he has done and finds it very good, for he has given sway to his wishes and inclinations. But his neighbor comes and searches him out, to tear down what he has built up and sell what he has bought, and his reins ponder and his heart grows sour to debase the assurance which the other has increased. Because not all hearts are equable, many are the workers of iniquity and the speakers of evil.

57

He-Goat & Lion

BEWARE OF HIM THAT GIVETH
COUNSEL FOR HIS OWN ADVANTAGE,
AND OF THINE ENEMY WHEN HE
MAKETH HIS PALATE SWEET.

A HE-GOAT was wandering astray on the tooth of a
sheer cliff where no shoots or grass was to be found,
for brimstone and salt had scorched all the land. A lion at
the foot of the mountain over against him perceived the
goat and said to him: "What ails thee that thou hast gone
up to a place of withered herbage? Thy folly thou hast set
on high; when the herbage of thy plain is sere thou hast
made thy dwelling on the heights, in a waterless land,
thirsty and weary. Come down with me into large pastures and the fruit thereof shall be for meat. It is a place
where lie rams and goats and fat kine, a joy of wild asses,
a pasture of flocks. My young and theirs find delight in
deep peace; they make their children lie down together.
Say not that there is grass and seed in thy place: Woe to
them who say of the evil that it is good and of the good
that it is evil." Said the goat: "I know, verily I know, that
with me there is no grass or seed and in thy place is the
beauty of Sharon and Carmel to heal the weary and
brokenhearted; before thy words reached me I had con-
templated descending thither to graze. But now that I have
heard thy counsel I have repented, for thou art he who
hath wounded many a head in the land. Better is a dry
crust and tranquillity therewith than the shaking of the
environs at the sound of thy voice, when thou comest to
shed blood and destroy souls."

The parable teaches understanding and admonishes if the imaginations of your heart are barren of understanding. If your enemy makes his palate sweet to entice you, beware of him who advises you for his own advantage. See and understand the tale of the goat, whose heart was not persuaded by the counsel of the lion who thought in his cunning to make him a prey, but understood that the advice was a deception. And the sage hath said: "Do wholly as he that loves thee advises; hear what thine enemy advises, but do it not." The words of thy friend, bring near like sapphires and emeralds; the words of thine enemy, hear, but do the reverse. If thy neighbors are without counsel and mute as a tree and thou findest none to consult, turn away from that counsel which is nearest thy desires and thou shalt be secure, for there is hope.

58

Boy & Man

A PERVERSE GENERATION ARE THEY
THAT PAY THE PRICE OF PEACE WITH WAR.

A LAD was walking innocently in the forest when the east wind began to storm and rage. His hands snuggled in his bosom, for he was chilled with the blast. Ice was cast forth like morsels, and there was snow and hail. He longed for the warmth of fire, for who could withstand the frost? A man of the forest who dwelt among the bushes saw him and took pity on him, and said: "There is sufficient for the burning, and the blaze is large." He urged the lad until he came to his house, and spoke upon his heart as though he were his kinsman and redeemer. And he covered him with garments, but he was not warmed. Before he came thither he had blown the breath of his mouth and nostrils upon his nails to dispel the chill of his hands. The man apportioned him food, for that his eye took pity upon him, and brought of his drink to strengthen his spirit. And the lad accepted of them and grew warm. He gave the lad liquor to share with him, but when he put it to his lips he could not drink it because of its great heat, so he breathed upon his wine goblet with his breath to cool it. Said the man in anger: "Quickly depart hence; a man such as thou I do not desire in my midst. This morning didst thou blow upon thy hands to dispel the chill, and this evening thou blowest upon thy warm wine to cool it. Far be it from me to make a friend and comrade of so perverse a mouth as thine. Verily I will cut thee off from the company of the upright in heart."

The parable is for flatterers who are not honest but have two hearts and many faces. They pay the price of peace with war, for they are a perverse generation. Out of each proceedeth flattery, and their chief desire and hope is to speak to their neighbor with cajolery and enticement. Iniquity and injustice are under their tongue. After they have spoken the pleasure of their soul and the desire of their heart, they mock and overturn the words they have spoken. Their hearts within them are not steadfast; therefore their reasoning standeth not fast, for the sense in their mouth is not firm. If they prevail in the earth there is no faith. The swallowing of words is as a plague in the chambers of the belly, as a sledgehammer that crusheth rock. A man shall desire in his midst only one formed in his own image.

59

Lion & Toad

THOU SHALT SURELY SAY TO MEN
OF MIGHT THAT THE GREAT MUST
BEWARE OF THE SMALL.

THE LION, whose strength surpassed all, was sleeping in the shade of a rock in the wilderness, and behind him in a cleft of the rock there stood a toad. Said the toad: "Who is this before my hole?" He knelt and crouched like a lion, and was moved with choler, and dashed up to him in the fury of his spirit; he bit the lion upon the forehead like an adder, and the lion awoke from his sleep. His eyes were like coals, and like flames they roved abroad to see who and where he was whose heart emboldened him to do such a thing. The toad had already returned by the way he had come; he looked at the lion, and behold, he was raging and furious, as if he would lop his biter down with terror. The toad called to him: "Art thou seeking him who hurt thee? It is I, the toad who stands before thee, that bit thee in my furious anger. I am greatly vexed that I did not kill thee. Alas for thee that thou hast sinned; thy sins will find thee out. Suddenly they shall rise up that shall bite thee, and they that shall vex thee shall awake. Wilt thou be my persecutor in thy strength and stature because I am accounted puny and contemptible in thy sight? Thou hast neared my rock to stop the entry to my house, and in my anger I have come forth to be thy persecutor."

The parable is to admonish the great with respect to the small, lest by reason of their strength and might and power and pride they sin against those smaller than they.

106

For the pursued are tenacious of life, and though they be small, the might of their heart is great. Within themselves they set their ambush to take vengeance in spite. The vain should be wise, for a giant is sometimes strangled by a fly, and there are times when towering giants stumble into pitfalls, and lions fear sheep.

60
Bullock & Ox

SWEETER IS THE SLEEP OF THE
TOILER THAN OF THE IDLER.

A BULLOCK saw an ox at his ploughing, and the hand of the husbandman was heavy upon him and placed fetters and rods upon him so that he could not move his neck. When the ox turned from the road, the bullock said to him: "Thy covenant with peace shall be disannulled by reason of excess of toil and labor. I am like a wild ass that runneth upon the way of the forest, in the path of the vineyards, and I have not been worked nor borne a yoke; I walk in the olive orchard amidst its foliage like a swift dromedary traversing her ways." The ox answered and said, with words of knowledge and in level speech: "All the while that labor presses heavy upon me and I am in bondage to the field and draw the yoke with all my strength, I rest secure and my soul liveth. But do thou not trust thy life, for that they have set thee free to be well-fed and fat, that thy neck hath not been subjected to much toil, that thou dost rest both at ploughing time and harvest, suddenly the chief of the butchers will take thee. Thou art indeed surrounded by snares." And it came to pass at the end of a month that a numerous folk came after the bullock and dragged him by ropes upon his neck, and they beat him to make him go and terrified him. While the ox ploughed his furrow with a song, the bullock was thrashed and tormented without mercy. The ox called to him: "Better for thee to have worked the earth than to go to the court of death, for from thy fall there is no rising."

The parable is for a man who labors heavily at the yoke to supply his need. Sweet is the sleep of the toiler, and his righteousness will be revealed in the congregation, for there is hope for his latter day. Not so the way of the sluggard. He prophesies that he will be saved without labor or toil, but he knows not his time, like the fish that are caught in a net.

61

Lion & Dog

BETTER TO LACK FOOD AND
RAIMENT THAN TO BE BOUND
TO THE TABLE OF ANOTHER.

A LION that had grown lean of the fat of his flesh, so that only bones and skin were left upon him, went upon his way slowly and without strength. There met him a fat dog, who mocked him and said: "Whither goest? Why art thou so meager, prince? Easy it were for thee to be among men and keep guard for them, to carry their burdens and serve them as a slave. Then wouldst thou not eat bread with scarceness and not suffer want, but eat flesh to thy heart's content, even as I who am become their servant and am waxed fat and thick and cov-

ered with flesh, instead of thy being meager of flesh and a wanderer by the way, pursued by the east wind and swept on by the blast. Even when they bind me with ropes and fetters, flesh and wheaten bread are given me for my repast; never has my expectation of my wonted fare been disappointed. My yoke is dissolved because of my fatness, and the bondage of my chains is love." Answered the lion: "Thy pride is the pride of one sated with bread, therefore dost thou not discern between thine honor and thy disgrace. Such a dog as thou are proud of speech; in thy hand is the custom of thy fathers who were bound to flocks of sheep to keep them, and fixed by a nail to the crib of an ass. Shall I be like you, bound with chains? Far be it from me to hear the crying of the driver! Better for me to be without a ruler and meager of fatness than to be a willing slave for the sake of abundant food, for if now my hand falls short of salvation, it is better for me to endure my affliction and my misery and to be free as my father was than to be a slave and dine on loaves of bread.

The parable: Thus shall it be done to the man whom the king delighteth to honor—to take prudent instruction and his admonition from the lion. Let his flesh be poor in fat, but let his honor not be poor, lest he acquire a master over himself and quench the light of his glory. Let him not boast of the fatness of his belly and the stoutness of his back and of the fatness wherewith he hath covered his face when he hath been crammed by the food of others. Better to be among those of small power, without abundant food and clothing, than to be bound to the table of others. Can a prudent man esteem himself lightly? Can he who doeth such things prosper and be delivered? He is trampled upon like a slave with ear bored; upon his garb is violence and beneath him a bed of shame. And the sage hath said: "A sufficiency which keepeth a man from vileness is better than money which bringeth him to shame and humiliation."

62

Wolves, Goats, Dog

HE THAT GIVETH THE SWORD FROM
HIS HAND TO HIS ENEMY GIVETH
HIM HIS DAY OF DOOM.

THE WOLVES, each proud and lofty in his heart, fought with the goats and their keeper the dog. The strength of the dog and the goats prevailed, and the lowly vanquished the stalwart; their hand smote the wolves, and the strong were as tow. The wolves sighed and groaned, and the goats whistled and gnashed their teeth at them. Then said the wolves to the goats with cunning guile: "We shall not go forth against you to war any more. With this only shall we be contented: that ye will hearken and be like ourselves and we shall no more rouse up battle against you if ye will give us a hostage and inform us when ye disperse and when ye wish to assemble. Then will wolf dwell with sheep or goat, and your righteousness shall be recompensed in the earth, and there shall be a covenant of peace between us and between you forever." The goats consented and said: "Whom of us will ye choose for yourselves to be a hostage in your hands? We are eager for your fellowship." Answered the wolves with guileful heart: "We ask of you only the dog." So the goats summoned the dog and gave him for a hostage; but for them this was for a sorrow, as if they had given up the ghost. For the dog had fought at their side, and all followed him as a marshal. He would say: "Stand steadfast, and deliverance shall spring up; I will heap evils upon them. Stand and fight after my example; let no neighbor say, I have waxed faint." Always he had strengthened their spirit, but now hope and victory were lost, for the wolves made battle upon them and smote them and crushed them to desolation.

The parable: Let not a man minish what is in his hand, to augment his enemy who wishes his downfall. His heart's sorrow takes root when he puts a sword in his enemy's hand wherewith to slay him. He that doeth these things is smitten with blindness; he debases the one and exalts the other. He that giveth foolishly is captured or crushed, and he that receiveth is mighty in his course and prevails.

63
Cock & Hen

THEY THAT PURSUE REWARDS AND
BRIBERY SOMETIMES QUARREL TOGETHER.

A COCK borrowed a bushel of wheat from a hen and
brought it from her house in scarves and wimples.
But the appointed day upon which the cock had agreed to
repay the loan passed, and he neither came nor asked an
extension of the term. Said she to him: "Surely thou wilt
faithfully repay the bushel as of yesterday, though it is
passed; buy the truth, and sell it not." Said he to her: "Far
be it from me to falsify my faith. The wheat is stored up
in heaps in my house; come with me to my house and I
shall pay it out by measure; for no precious gain would I
defraud thee." Said she to him: "Lo, guile sprouteth in
thy spirit. I call upon thee in the presence of my brethren
and thine: Return the wheat in the place thou hast received it, so that my chicks can gather the grains that fall
from thy measuring. Starvation hath well-nigh slain them,
and they say to their mother, Where is corn? For their
hand is waxed feeble and they are in want. Now they can
gather what hath been scattered; therefore I bid thee bring
the grain to my boundary, so that those dependent upon
my food may find the corn that falls." Said the cock:
"Nay, with what is scattered and spread abroad thou shalt
not sustain thy soul and the soul of thy children. Rather
shall I measure the grain in my tent: Rise, hearken to my
voice. There my host shall eat that which shall fall before /
your eyes, even as thou hast thought to do for thy children."

The parable is drawn from advocates and judges who

debase justice and righteousness. Some that pursue rewards and accept bribes quarrel together when a suit comes before them, and they murmur in their tents, saying: "This suit shall be in my house and court, and no whit of my honor and dignity shall fall to the ground." And the other saith: "Nay, but in my boundary and threshold; and it shall be heard only at my word." This they do only to receive bribes and to subvert justice by deception and trickery. None cries out for justice and none judges in good faith, and not one rouses himself to make justice strong but only to grind it fine. He that wishes fills his hand and makes his words crooked. Woe to him that coveteth evil gain for his house!

64

A Bird Buildeth Her Nest
in the Grain

BE DEAF OF HEARING, BLIND OF
SEEING, MUTE OF SPEAKING; THEN
WILT THOU ASCEND ON STAIRS
AND MAKE THEE STRONG.

A BIRD had made her nest in the standing grain, and when harvest time appeared she continued living there as was her wont, the mother brooding over her chicks. They said to her: "We have heard them saying to the messenger: 'Put ye in the sickle, for the harvest is ripe.' " Dread entered the heart of the bird; she was afflicted, tossed with tempest, and not comforted, and she said to them: "Before the sun sets I shall know whether they will raise the scythe against the standing grain." She went in the footsteps of the master of the field, going and returning, and seemed like a bird gone astray from its nest. Before he returned to his house she hovered before him, and she heard him beseech his neighbors: "Be ye prepared to come to my assistance upon the third day in the portion of field which is mine to reap my harvest." But they would not hearken unto him, and the man returned to his tent heavy and displeased. She sighed no more as she returned to her house; the mother of sons rejoiced. Said she: "The soles of our feet shall not trouble alien and brackish waters like birds astray from a castaway nest. I have heard their secret; the foot of man shall not pass over it. Lodge ye here, depart not; before the time comes when they reap, when the sickle masters the standing grain, the Lord will defend and deliver, pass over and preserve." Daily she went to hear what their counsel might be, and when the day came when his neighbors consented to aid him, she said: "Go forth from here, tarry not; fear and shun sickle and scythe."

The parable: When thou seest that respite hath come, for that thou dwellest in tranquillity and security; if then the ruler desire to raise his hand against thee, make thy spirit lowly, for it is better to yield to a man who hath helpers. And Solomon hath said: "Let the ways of instruction not depart from thine eyes." Be understanding and wise amongst thy neighbors, a deaf man that hears, a blind man that sees, a mute man that speaks; then shalt thou ascend by the steps of prudence and increase thy strength daily.

65
Lion & Ass

THE MAN THAT KNOWETH
NOT HIS OWN PLACE WILL
REVEAL HIS SHAME; HIS
HEART IS NOT WITH HIM.

A LION invited an ass to show him the choice splendors of his greatness, and the ass was proud in his heart, saying: "Who is as I am? To whom doth the king desire to show greater honor than to me, now that I go to join his company? Now they will call me the king's second, for he hath made me his suite; me hath he chosen, and no stranger, with him." And he said to the lion: "I shall cast my dread over the cattle; they shall tremble at my voice and flee at my rebuke." Answered the lion: "Make thy work lofty, let thy voice be heard on high. We shall go forth to spoil much prey, and thy face shall advance to the battle. Thou shalt roar and I shall rend; thou shalt seize the prey and I shall break its neck." So they went forth into the field and found sheep and steers and fat cattle, and set their goal to spoil and lay waste. Said the lion: "Make them hear the roar of thy voice; thunder upon them with my sound." The ass raised his voice, and the sound reverberated in their camp. At the sound all the ewes were scattered; at its lifting the rams were terrified. Panic fell upon the camp of those that walked on fours, and when they turned to flee, the lion spoiled and devoured and was sated with them. As they fled hither and thither with the noise of a great host, the lion said: "Make not thy voice heard longer; enough of thy thunder." When he had finished his spoiling, and the ass and the lion were standing beside a carcass, the ass said: "Surely thou hast heard the majesty of my braying and hast seen that my neck is decked with a mane. In thy wisdom thou wilt choose me, and at this time tomorrow I will frighten the cattle and cast their victory down to earth, for it is not to the king's profit to suffer them, neither them nor their bellowing. Now these are the judgments which thou shalt set before them. They shall flee at my rebuke and be terrified by it. We shall make our lips strong; who is lord over us? Hear me, my lord the king; surely my words shall find favor with one that walketh aright." The lion answered him: "Whoso knoweth thy generation from above and below will not be afraid of thy voice nor abase himself for its noise. Despised and lowly and stubborn creature, wilt thou spoil prey for the lion? Those that will become estranged from me will say in my ear, 'How hast thou spoiled the goats and not crushed the ass?'"

The parable is for an honored man who makes a despised and contemptible man his associate. The spirit of pride will sprout and be revealed in the latter when he boasts of his fellowship and recognizes not his lowliness. As the obstinacy of his heart is revealed, his tongue will utter large boasts: "Such and such have I done by my wisdom and understanding." And the sage hath said in his wisdom: "The fool's silence is his remedy."

66

Mule & Fox

WHEN A MAN IS ASKED HIS
NAME AND BIRTH IT DOTH NOT
ALWAYS SUIT HIS GLORY TO TELL
OF HIS FATHER AND MOTHER.

A MULE walking by the way was met by a fox who had never before seen him. The fox observed the majesty of his face and that his eyes were bright and his ears long, and said in his heart: "Who is this I now behold? What is the nature of this creature? I have never seen a picture like him, nor himself, until this moment. With his long ears stretching aloft he must be filled with wisdom and knowledge and shrewdness." The fox approached to hear his sayings and add cleverness to his own cleverness; perhaps he would obtain his confidence. He asked the mule who had given him birth, and the mule answered: "My uncle walked in pride; he was the horse upon whom the king rode. On the day of battle and destruction he leapt and pranced, and he pawed the earth with stormy passion. His neck was clothed with a mane, and his lordly neighing was terrible. His hoofs were like flint; they thirsted for hot battle and hungered for destruction. They never broke ranks but sped like sparks of fire, each shattering the rock like a sledgehammer. His eyes were like flame, like flashing lightning. He was a tower of strength for his rider and strode with neck outstretched. From afar he sniffed war and shouted for the enemy's destruction. He pursued and overtook all that rebelled against his rider. Such is the genealogy of the mule."

The parable is for a man magnificently attired from head to foot; there is no blemish in him, and he preens himself on his grandeur. But when they ask him his name and birth, because it suits not his splendor to tell of his father and mother, he mentions his relative who ennobles him, and makes no mention of him that begot him. Either his uncle or his cousin shall redeem him; it is their honor and glory that rise to his lips, their great deeds and their prowess. I have searched but never found a true man among those who say of father and mother, "I have never seen them," and who claim kinship with the great of the family, for that the family's glory has fallen away from his father and himself. And I, Berechiah, have said in my haste: "Woe to a man who is called 'of the family of Buzzi'; whoso has fallen from his fathers' merits, an untimely birth is better than he."

67

Two Apes & a Lion

WHEN DECEITFUL MEN ARE FILLED
WITH ENVY, EACH AROUSES
HATRED OF THE OTHER.

TWO APES came before their king, the lion, each seeking a gift. The lion perceived that the one would make objection to what the other would say, for the one was covetous and the other envious, so he said to them: "If ye look to me to ask something of mine, I shall give you as ye ask me, but my consent is on condition that ye heed my voice; one of you shall reveal his request to my ear, and after he hath spoken, I shall not recant but grant his petition. The second, if his mouth and tongue remain silent until the first have done with his request, I shall esteem so highly as to give him twofold my gift to his fellow, for I shall desire his honor and dignity." The covetous one spoke cunning guile in his heart: "I shall surely remain silent; to do so will be wisdom on my part. I shall hear what my fellow will ask and what speech he will utter, and I shall obtain twice what accrues to him." And it came to pass when he fell silent and hearkened, that the envious one said in his heart: "My fellow who is silent shall not be accounted wise; I am as clever as he and no less prudent. Though he be wise he shall procure evil." So the envious one called to the king, saying: "The utterance of thy lips thou shalt keep, and thou shalt do as thou hast spoken in my ears. I ask of thee to pierce one of my eyes. Lo, I have revealed my desire to thine ears; would that my request be fulfilled." Said the lion: "I shall heed thy voice and fulfill thy petition, nor shall I forsake thee until I have done that which I have spoken unto thee." And to the covetous one he said: "Lo, I will take from thee thy two eyes; thou must surely understand what is before thee." And he rendered them requital for their guile and gave them their request.

The parable is for contentious men who are filled with envy. One arouses hatred against the other; one says in his heart: "How hath my neighbor been uplifted and exalted? I shall smite him with my tongue and not leave him root or branch, for to me he is briars and thorns. Rather than that any of my intention fall to the ground I shall give fields and vineyards and houses; let my soul die with the Philistines." He is stranger to himself in order to harm his neighbor; his profit is as a purse of holes. In their hearts they search out deceits and pitfalls and trickery and plots. Even if the king should say to them: "Make your counsel sweet together; wherefore should I be bereft of you both in a single day?"—they have ears that hear not, for they have strayed far from the path of prudence. Until that one hath broken and destroyed the wealth of his neighbor, the child shall behave himself proudly against the ancient and the base against the honorable. And the sage hath said: "Shun the envious man when he sees thee; he will mourn for thy joy and prosperity."

Lion, Man, Pit, Snake

THE TIME IS SHORT AND THE
WORK MUCH AND THE MASTER
OF THE HOUSE IS PRESSING.

A LION went up from his lair to the crossroads of the highway, awaiting and lurking for his prey from morning till evening, to take it in his drag. An innocent passerby saw the lion roar, and trembled with fear and anxiety, for the lion charged upon him furiously, resolved to spoil him. Finding death bitter, the man ran toward a pit amidst clay cisterns; the pit was empty, there was no water in it. In the midst of the wall of the pit he found spikes extending from this side and that and was glad of them, for his feet stood upon the spikes; he thought he had found a refuge and escape from the lion who had lorded it over him and that he had escaped forever from slaughter, so that his footsteps would never be moved. But at the extremity of the pit he saw lurking a fiery poisonous serpent awaiting to swallow him alive, like the abyss, and his terror was redoubled. In the midst of noonday his shadow was as the night; tribulations poured over him without surcease. He had escaped the lion but encountered the serpent, who opened his mouth wide to swallow him. If he eluded the lion, the asp's tongue would slay him, for after the lion he was faced by the serpent. Said he: "Alas, who shall live? If I ascend, the lion will smite me; if I descend, the serpent's tongue will be my grave. Whence cometh my help between the two camps of lion and serpent? Furthermore, lack of bread and all sustenance hath afflicted me with cleanness of teeth, and I can find no water. But this is my comfort: I have found a faithful footing and rods of strength to support my feet until the lion depart from upon me. I shall take my stand upon them like a mighty man and shall not descend to the edges of the pit." As he spoke thus in his heart a rat emerged from over him, and he looked upon it and perceived that there was no black hair in it but only white. From the other side, opposite the hole, there emerged a rat wholly black. They put their teeth to the spikes upon which the man's feet were standing and gradually gnawed them away; day by day they destroyed his support. When the man saw that the spikes were weakened and shaking, three were the afflictions that beset him, and he lamented for his misfortunes: "Woe for the lion, woe for the serpent before whom my foot is apprehensive; woe for the two rats who gnaw away my standing place; woe for thirst, woe for hunger. Speedily I shall be for a mockery, and my soul will be humbled by the pit and by my torments. There is but a step between death and me, and I shall never return to see my comrade. In the darkness have I spread my couch, and it is thou, thou pit of gloom, in whose boundary I stand. If I am famished I shall not say unto thee: 'Shall I bring forth my bread and the manna of my sustenance from the rock?'" When he had so spoken twice and had not forgotten his plaint, as if he were in the pouch of a sling, the Rock whose power is over all gave him honey to suck from the flint, and said: "Open thy mouth and eat, and thou shalt not lack all thy days. Honey hast thou found; eat thy fill and take pleasure in its goodness and richness." With honey and milk beneath his tongue he stripped off the terror wherewith he had clothed himself and said: "What is sweeter than honey?" He forgot what was above him and what below, and that he was sitting in darkness, what was before him and what behind, the white rat and the black who were thrusting him from his perch and banishing him from the world; he did not remember the lion above him nor the serpent under his feet, but found delight in the honey which he ate as it were wheat of Minnith and Pannag. Wafers made with honey did he taste. But Jeshurun waxed fat and kicked; and when he had grown fat and portly, the rats who had daily gnawed his standing place removed his goodness from him. Suddenly the spikes were broken and cut off from the hole of the pit and from the wall, in deed, not in word. As either spike was severed and fell, the man who had stood upon them reached the edge of the pit and the mouth of the serpent that heeded no enchantment. Never again did he see his house and his people, and his place knew him no more.

The parable is goodly instruction for the soul, to clothe oneself in the raiment of freedom. The lion that approaches is death, which, as it were, lurks for a man and never turns its back nor lies down until it has devoured its prey. The pit is the world in which he stands. He flies to the pit that he be not seized, and every stranger there is a permanent sojourner in his own sight. He regards himself firmly fixed as a spike, to live long and see seed. The evil inclination in the heart of man is the serpent below him with its mouth open toward him, which always cries, "Give, give! Now shalt thou despise what thou hast loved." The rat wholly white is the day which gives him light, and the black rat, the night; together they combine to consume man utterly. As man proceeds toward the cemetery, they circle round and about him, for they are pledged to destroy his standing place and thrust him away. But he does not perceive his end; the honey which makes him oblivious to all this is the pleasure of the world, which suffuses his soul, and the delightful pastimes which spread a net for his feet. It causes his joy to flourish and his calamity to crumble, and its taste is as of a wafer made with honey. But while he is intent upon his dainties the roots of this joy wither in an instant, and the height of his harvest is broken; he lies with his fathers, whose dwelling place is the grave. The wise man who has indited sage sayings and linked them together into a chain has said: "The pleasure of this world is honey smeared over poison." I render my creator thanksgiving and praise for sustenance and livelihood. For one who does not as I do, his day is trouble and perplexity. In the midst of their food is a stone, for they have filled their teats with milk and have murmured in their tents, and have not taken thought to praise their creator and shepherd.

And I plied my poesy and said:

> Lion is death, the pit a serpent which heedeth no
>   enchantment;
> The white rat the day; the black, the night. My
>   heart perceiveth
> They are pledged to end the life they symbolize,
> As the pit symbolizes the world. His foot rests on
>   delusion.
> His world is as a wafer of honey, but its fruit is
>   deceptive.
> The spike of the pit breaks, and he dies.
> Not with fleeces is he then covered.

69

Wolf, Fox, Dove

THE FELLOWSHIP OF FLATTERERS
AND THE PERVERSE IS ALWAYS
FOR EVIL.

THE WOLF, the fox, and the dove entered into a faithful covenant to spoil prey for their food and to divide their booty equally. Together they came to a covert, for the shadows of evening were falling, but found only a bat, which they brought forth from the holes in the dust and the reeds; and so they returned hungry and weary. Said the fox: "How can our booty be divided? If it be slaughtered will it suffice us? We walked in the desert, the mountain, and the lowland; but the dove found no resting place for the sole of her foot. But it is fitting that we give her her portion, that she be not robbed amongst us and that we deal not deceitfully with her. Come, let us cast lots. He that first telleth his age and prove elder than his comrade, we will hearken to his voice and give him the bat." Now the other two were not so old as he and would be deprived of the booty. Said the two: "Thy counsel is good and just." So they cast lots, and the lot fell upon the dove; said she: "Though I have toiled with you and not found a resting place, I am the dove that came forth from Noah's ark. Amidst the strong I divide prey and cleave it asunder; the wings of the dove are silvery with age." Said the fox: "I am old, and none can tell the number of my years. But from my fathers of ancient days I have received by tradition a sign for ascertaining the number of years that have passed from the day of my birth: The white hairs upon me are my witness; each hair represents a year. If the truth be sought, the number of my years is beyond calculation."

The wolf answered in anger and said: "Fox and dove, hearken to my words. There is none beside me older than I, for I am hoary and full of years. The sign of my age is neither whiteness nor redness. If I count my years they are more numerous than the sands. I have labored to ascertain and have discovered that when I passed two years I reached the third, but I know not the last nor the first. Who will instruct me and bid me leave the bat to one smaller than I?" So he ate it before their eyes and left them not a morsel.

The parable is for flatterers and deceivers, froward men who work iniquity, who bring people near with their lips but keep them far from their reins. If a man have business with them, they reply with soft humility and shamefacedness, but the paths of uprightness depart from their eyes. Widows are their prey and they rob orphans, but with their lips they say: "My will is bound by His will, to do what is good and upright." If one is involved in a suit and is judged and the judge says, "Pay," then he is deaf to words he desires not to hear. He gnashes his teeth and speaks angrily and arouses all his wrath, for he is confident, like a strong man in his strength, in provoking robbery and destruction and in walking ways that are crooked. So did the wolf to the dove and the fox: He made his counsel sweet with them and in the end dealt treacherously and took their portion against their will and smote them as if they were wicked. But they that sow the truth will reap sevenfold their portion and will shine over against the light. Before me it is inscribed and before me sealed that the guilty must pay and innocent win merit.

70

Lion & Cattle

IT IS GOOD TO APPEASE BY
SWEETNESS OF LIPS IN ORDER
TO PREVENT COALS OF HATRED
FROM WORKING DESTRUCTION.

THE LION was strong among the cattle, and his teeth
were encompassed with awe. Among the sheep he
caused widowers and mourners, and turned not back before anyone. To the north and to the right he fought; he
was cruel and showed no mercy. Even when they fled before him, he confounded them with the terror of his roar.
The archers hated him and shot at him and wounded him,
once in the belly and once in the back; his hand was against
every man, and every man's hand, against him. He pitied
none that walked on fours except the deer and the camel.
All the cattle in their fright cursed him with mighty curses
when they hid themselves from before him and took shelter in the crevices of the rock. But the deer and the camel
were his comrades and departed not from the land of his
dwelling; each made his heart kindly and restrained those
that cursed him. But the persecuted cursed and wept, and
while all cursed the lion, the deer and the camel blessed
him. They called to the cattle and the beasts: "Ye that
graze in the fields and in desert reaches, it is because ye
curse him that he arouses all his wrath against you. If ye
turn the curse to a blessing, great advantage will accrue to
you. Do as we do and it will be proven that ye will find
favor in his eyes and he will no longer smite you, but give
you his covenant of peace. Behold, and do as we do; our
peace he hath not disturbed." They hearkened to the

counsel, and the lion rested his hand and was appeased.

The parable is to prevent coals of hatred from working destruction, and to appease an enemy by sweetness of counsel. Foolish indeed is he who storms, and kindles wrath against wrath. Who thinks to murder is murdered; who vanquishes wickedly is vanquished. If thou abominate and curse thine enemy, thou wilt ever desecrate thine own honor. Consider the ways of the Rock, whose works are always perfect; never are his loving-kindnesses ended or exhausted. He cursed the serpent and made his bread the dust; but wherever the serpent goes, his bread is with him—whether he ascends or descends he is in no fear for his provision. He cursed the woman in her youth, but all men run after her. He cursed the earth which he established, but all are sustained by it. He cursed the slave because he was shameless, but he eats and drinks as does the master. Hear instruction; let it be firmly established and builded, and thou wilt walk and rest secure. And the sage hath said: "Though thy excellency mount up to the heavens and thine enemy is bowed down before thee, he will make thee sin with evil thoughts."

And I plied my poesy and said:

Wherefore should man of tongue rage when the
    Rock hath not raged,
Wherefore should the generation be in terror of thy
    mouth?
His she-ass the swordless Balaam availed not to slay
    with his tongue,
What time he went forth to curse the people.

71

Starling & Princess

A MAN FILLED WITH WISDOM AND
KNOWLEDGE HATH AN OBSERVANT
EYE AND AN ATTENTIVE EAR.

A PRINCESS raised a starling and taught him to speak
plainly and brought him to her chamber in her father's house, in her youth. In clear speech and pretty wit
the starling was cleverer than all the birds, and he understood, when he heard news, that there is a time for speaking and a time for remaining silent. But he could not go
and come, and his heart grieved. She had made him a cage
of iron reeds, and amongst the reeds his voice was heard.
One day a knight who intended to cross the sea came to
the court of the king and queen and commended his
house and sons and land to the queen. Her palate was
smoother than oil, and she said: "I will surely hearken to
thy voice and keep mine eye over all that is thine." The
starling understood that the knight sought to cross the sea
and as he passed his cage called him by name and said to
him: "Lo, thou wilt cross the sea; I shall speak glorious
things of thee. If thou see a bird in my form and likeness,
be mindful of me and give him greeting in my name, and
graciously and mercifully ask him counsel how I may go
forth from my barred prison. My soul is wearied of it, for
I am surrounded by hedge and wall. Neither have I of-
fended here, but I was stolen from my family and shut up
amongst men. Deal with me in kindness and truth. He
that is pent in prison is considered as one dead; I am pent
and cannot go forth, and my food will have no savor until
I am free. Then will I lift up my head. Therefore I adjure
thee to recall me to thine acquaintance and upon thy re-

turn to tell me the words of his responses." The knight
departed thence and went down to the sea. Flying toward
him was a bird of the form of him that had spoken to him,
and before he approached, he raised his voice and said to
him: "A bird of your form and likeness who dwells
amongst men and is pent up in their barred gaol sends you
his greeting. He hath adjured me to ask counsel of thee
how he may redeem his soul and go forth from his prison
cell. Deliverance will not fail him if he can again appear in
the forest and change his prison garb." When he had finished speaking, the bird folded his wings and fell upon
the knight in a swoon, as if death had swept him away.
The knight took him up and put his eyes to his own, to
restore his breath, and sprinkled fresh water upon his face,
and then put him in his bosom; mayhap he would grow
warm. When he saw there was no hope he threw him
away; his heart grieved, and he knew not what had ailed
him. Then he departed quickly, to proceed to his desired
destination, and returned to his family in the city of his
dwelling. The king received him joyfully on his return
and embraced and kissed him. As the starling paced back
and forth he perceived that the knight was returned from
his journey and asked him whether he had remembered
his life of sorrow, whether he had found a bird of his likeness, what he had done and what he had said to him. The
knight recounted all that had befallen: that it had been a
day of wrath for the bird when he heard his words—how
his plans were cut short, for with no hunter or fowler he
had fallen dead on the field; that he had sprinkled him
with water, to return his breath, and covered him with
garments, without his growing warm; that before his
stink and ill savor should come up, he had cast him away
in revulsion. The starling listened attentively. When the
princess came to her chamber and did not hear the bird
chirping, her wrath burned in her. She opened the cage
and saw him, and sent her handmaiden to take him up.
He was lying as one dead, and she was vexed when she

saw that he stirred no wing, as if paralysis had seized him; where he crouched, there he lay. She threw water upon his head: perchance she could restore his soul; and she took him and put him in her lap. But he neither rose nor moved, and she abode in silence. Then she cast him from her hands to the ground, wet her face with the tears of her eyes, bewailed and lamented him, and departed from his side weeping. When the bird heard that she had gone, all his wishes were attained; he spread his wings and flew, and his pinions wearied not of flight.

The parable: A man filled with wisdom and knowledge hath a seeing eye and an attentive ear. He hears what men say abroad, and his eyeballs look straight before him. Before others perceive his plans he is quick to begin and complete them, in give and take, in purchase and sale. Like the starling he will be diligent and prosper. He who reflects in his wisdom and proceeds accordingly, cometh forth from prison to reign.

And I plied my poesy and said:

A man of sense is praised for his sense; and a fool,
   reviled for his folly.
There are wise men who are so openly, not in riddles,
And there are simpletons wrapped in a cloak of folly.
Folly fits close, and moves not, though continually
   reviled;
But a hint suffices for the course of the perceptive,
And his understanding is proven by his acts.
So the starling fell as one slain and won his life for his
   prize.

72

Ram & Ten Ewes

THERE IS NO FAITH ON THE LIPS
OF THE ENVIOUS, FOR HIS STOCK
IS FALSEHOOD.

A RAM had ten ewes, who took delight in his company.
He loved the two who were without peer in the
flock, and neither was barren; but if he approached one he
aroused envy and sorrow in the heart of the other. One
saw that he loved her fellow more than herself, and
Rachel [ewe] was envious of her sister. Her tongue was as
an arrow shot out, she uttered slander against her, she trod
her bow for falsehood—for the dagger of envy pierced her
heart. Said she to the ram: "Thy spouse taketh newcomers
each morning; she receiveth strangers instead of her husband; a ram other than her husband has lain with her, to
seduce her from thee and make her obedient to him;
willingly she revels in his shadow; in the evening she
goeth and in the morning returneth, and how canst thou
show her compassion? Her filthiness is in her skirts; her
sentence is beheading. In the lust of her soul she hath
snuffed up the wind, to separate from thee in her harlotry. Her uncleanness is within her; let the scum be
cleansed away." Such words of falsehood and treachery
did she speak, and added many similar words to their
number. Answered the ram: "I do not believe thy saying,
for I know that boldness and shamelessness are under thy
tongue. Thou hast imagined evil things in thy heart and
hast spoken lies against her in thy hatred and envy of her,
which pervert ways of uprightness. If thy soul were bound
to her soul with an eternal love ready and watchful in all
things, then had I attended to thy saying. But as long as

life is in me I will keep afar the slanderous woman moved by hatred and envy; I will not reward hypocritical mockers at the feast with a cake.

The parable: If a man speak against his fellow according to his wickedness, thou shalt be wise if thou fairly investigate whether the words are sound; for if his fellow be turned to his enemy, thou wilt understand that in willfulness hath he spoken. But if he loves him as his life and has never caused him hurt, consider that the thing is true and the heart of the second, purer and more innocent than the first. The arrows of slander are sharpened with coals of broom. The words of a talebearer are as wounds, and turn love to its opposite; and a whisperer separateth chief friends.

And I plied my poesy and said:

Keep afar the talebearer that separates loving friends
And hurls the arrow of slander like lightning;
His heart is bitter though his palate is sweet,
And his lips compound hypocrisy. Scorn the willful
Who kiss thee with their mouth, while within them
Rivers of hatred flow deep. They cleave close
On the day of your joy, but speedily distant
On the day of calamity shalt thou find them.

73
Flea & Camel

HATRED IS INSCRIBED FOR THE
POOR MAN; THE RICH MAN LOOKS
UPON HIM WITH THE EYE OF ENMITY.

A FLEA mounted a camel. The camel went upon his
way to traverse a large stretch of land, and the flea
was hidden in the wool of his neck; the camel bore him
upon his shoulder and knew not of his lying down or
rising up. When he came to the end of his boundary, the
flea fell at his feet and wept and besought him not to grow
angry for his trouble, for his goodness and kindness overwhelmed him and he would be his slave in all places. The
camel answered: "How have I benefited thee, and where
have I seen thee?" Said he to him: "On thy shoulder hast
thou borne me, and I have reached my desired destination,
thanks to thee, who hast been willing to carry me. The
sole of my foot hath not essayed to touch the ground. For
that thou hast brought me hither, peace and long life be
thine." Answered the camel: "Woe is me that thou hast
laid the burden of thy yoke upon me! Abhorred and
abominated art thou, though thou raise thy nest high as
the eagle. How wert thou not afraid to rest upon me? Prepare thy steps for flight. Is it seemly for me to bring near
me one of thy form and image? On the day thou seest my
face again thou shalt die. Woe for the day I was so heavy-
laden and burdened; from carrying thee my back is become chafed." So was the flea dismissed by the camel,
whom it cost no effort to carry him.

The parable is for a poor man who consults the rich

man's peace and honor. He expresses his gratitude for a service which is no deprivation to the rich but benefits the poor. Into the rich man's heart it pours bitterness; and in return for love he hates the poor man and turns his face from him and looks upon him with the eye of enmity. For hatred of the poor is inscribed in the heart of the rich.

74

Stag & Dogs

HE WHO BOASTS OF HIS GREAT MIGHT
WILL FALL, AND NONE WILL HELP HIM.

WHEN the stag, desiring to slake his thirst, came to a running stream, he cast his eye upon the water and from his reflection observed that he possessed antlers. Said he: "I am rich. I have discovered my might. Who can compare with me to win praise like my praise? My horns are not like the horns of an ox but are planted in the plain of my forehead and arranged like ascending stairs. Both are perfect in grace and beauty. He who stands over against me, for him sentence of death is digged and hewn. Any with whom I quarrel, I can gore with them, to the west and to the north." As his feet strayed in the water, lo, a brace of dogs were tarred against him by their master. The stag bethought him to flee in haste; he ran not to the highroad and level ground but into the dense forest, amid thickets of thorns. His counsel tripped him and he stumbled in his pride, for when he set his face toward the branches, lo, he was caught by his horns in the thicket, and there the dogs and the hunters butchered him. So he was destroyed through his antlers, which were his pride;

pride goeth before a fall. Like them all his limbs were delivered to be carved up, though in his sight they were the
fairest of all.

The parable: Let thine eyes see and thine ears hear; and
fear not to approach the tree of knowledge, lest thou be
hasty in thy thoughts and embrace all that is right in thine
eyes. For ofttimes that which thou dost approach and
choose by thine imagination is like the fury of sea serpents
and the heads of asps; if by reason of love and pride thou
stumble by them, that which thou hast considered solid
footing for thy shoe will prove a gin and a snare. Let
strength and glory be supreme in thy heart.

75

Wolf & Shepherd

COUNT NOT THE KINDNESS YOU
CONFER UPON A MAN AS A DEBT.

A WOLF was pursued on his way, through desert,
mountain, and lowland, and in his great terror went
astray. He accosted a shepherd and said: "The tumult of
the chase is pursuing after me; I flee the sound of horse-
man and archer. They have spread a net to catch me, and
have gone to the right and to the left; they have risen to
the clouds and ascended the cliffs. Because a desert wolf
ravaged them, they said: 'Come, let us cut them off, that
no trace be left of them.' Would that thine eye take compassion upon me and not deliver me to the soul of mine
enemies! They rage to scatter me and have chased me from
the forest; they are gathered together under the nettles.
Do thou, who gatherest in the strayed, be my shelter from
before the ravager; let my soul be precious in thy sight.
Make not thy mouth large in the day of tribulation, and
let me hide until my pursuers turn back; they pant after
me to their heart's content. If I come now with thee I will
multiply their sorrow and send the tooth of beasts upon
them." Said the shepherd: "Go and hide in the cleft of the
mountains of Bether. I shall confuse the enemy's counsel
and deliver thee from the edge of the sword." So the wolf
ran to hide in the cleft of the rock, where he crouched and
bent low and was saved. The pursuers who wandered
astray after him came to the shepherd and said to him:
"Hast thou seen the wolf which has lain awake against our
cities and torn away an arm and even a head?" He answered them: "See his path; this is the way ye shall go.
Surround him, chase him, drive him from his covert;

hurry after him and catch him. Cursed be the man who withholds his sword from killing him." Every man that ran after him went astray, for their course was mistaken. When these grew weary, fresh hunters came from nearby, and each drew his sword. But the people labored in vain, for the shepherd had misled them with mouth and hand to point a road which led them astray. But his eye he had turned to the wolf, and his face toward the wolf's. When the pursuers turned back, wet with the showers of the mountains, the shepherd went to the wolf and said to him: "Arise and go thy way; I have fulfilled thy words and have not permitted my mouth to sin against thy flesh. I have given thee surcease of all thy sighing and have not suffered my palate to sin. I have delivered thee from descent to the pit. Be strong and of good courage; fear not and be not afraid." The wolf answered: "Thou hast done me great kindness with the word of thy mouth and the gesture of thy hand, in that thou didst teach my pursuers to go on crooked ways. My complaint is of thine eyes, for they looked at me steadily, without rest or respite. Thine eyes that looked straight were my troublers that would deliver me to my foes; with them wouldst thou have breached the wall, for thou didst look upon the land before thee, where I lay hidden. But for a little, I had been destroyed by thy gaze."

The parable: Let not your eyes be talebearers. If you speak of your comrade's deeds to a man and your words are judicious, take care not to turn toward your comrade, toward his aspect and stature, his form and image, for your eyes will communicate the words of your heart to his intelligence. With my ears I have heard the saying of the sage: "I made a covenant with mine eyes not to look upon a man when I speak of him." For from the look of my eyes he will understand in his heart. If I speak long of his shame or his grace while my eyeballs gaze straight at him, if he perceives it, the shame will be turned to abuse and the grace to flattery. And Solomon in his lofty wisdom hath said [Proverbs 10.10]: "He that winketh with the eye causeth sorrow."

And I plied my poesy and said:

Wise is he, except that when he deliberates concern-
ing a man
Thither his eye turns. Who speaks of pressed curds
Must not look to the cheese.

76

Sun & Moon

A MAN HEAVY WITH HONOR AND
POSSESSIONS IS NEVER SATISFIED
WITH THEIR EXTENT.

THE SUN, whose rule is by day, besought all living substance, requesting that the moon be given him for a companion. They answered him: "Thy hand is exceedingly strong and powerful; we shall not give thee a helpmeet. Lo, when thou art alone thou wreakest violence upon the snow: The sun waxeth warm and it melteth. When thou goest forth in thy strength, the king and his host are confounded: If the sun shine upon him he incurreth guilt. Thou goest forth from thy canopy like a bridegroom: Lo, thou hast dried up mighty rivers. Then how shall we join the moon to thee? Thou shalt not go with her, here nor there."

The parable is for a man who possesses wealth and riches and honor and cattle, and he desires to heap up as much again, to multiply what he hath and make him strong, for the might of his hand he finds insufficient. Do not consent to him, do not hearken to his voice to add forces to his force. Fitting is the instruction of wise Solomon [Proverbs 22.16]: "He that giveth to the rich surely cometh to want."

77

Viper & Man

KEEP AFAR HIM THAT COMES
NEAR THEE FOR THE SAKE OF
THY SILVER AND THY GOLD.

A MAN saw a viper and by the smoothness of his lips persuaded him to come into his boundaries. With great eloquence he besought him, until the viper hearkened to his voice and came round about his dwelling. When the man saw that he trusted him, he rejoiced and his heart was glad. He honored him greatly in his dwelling, and watched over him as the apple of his eye; he fed him to his satisfaction, with butter of kine and milk of goats. The viper too turned his desire to the man, until he told him he would show him his treasures. Thus for many days were they joined together and did not part from their love. The viper contrived a plan to test the man, to see whether his heart were just toward him; he called to the man and said: "My beloved, man after mine own heart, hearken unto me and I will reveal all my way, for thou art a man of mine own esteem. I shall return to my native land, to the sons of my people and my family, and I am resolved, good sir, to bring to you the most precious of my treasures, but thou must not lay thy hands upon it." He answered him: "I shall heed thy voice; thou shalt decree a thing and it shall be established unto thee." The viper went forth and brought the man an egg. Said he to him: "This egg is white and pure; no man knoweth its worth nor hath understanding of these matters, for it cannot be valued with the purest gold. If my soul be removed from thee, guard this egg from being cracked, for if so be that it is cracked, then is my hope perished. In thy hand I commit my spirit, for my welfare is bound up with it, so long as it is cared for and guarded." Then the viper departed, and the man rejoiced at his going. Quickly his heart fermented and he pondered iniquity upon his couch. He said to his wife, who shared his counsel: "This egg which has been entrusted unto us let us crack for ourselves, and there we shall find a treasure. Nor will our hand fall short, for the viper will lie smitten, and we shall fill our houses with booty." Even as they plotted so they committed evil. They cracked the viper's egg, and the liquid issued forth and spilt on the ground. Then were they ashamed of their counsel and found no profit in their deed. The viper returned from his travel to the inhabited city, the goal of his desire, and saw that the egg was cracked. Said he to the man: "Thy heart hath gone astray. For thy friendship I say, 'Woe is me that I have brought thee near to me and that I dwelt in thy midst until iniquity was discovered in thee.' Thou hast not desired my nighness but hast breached the wall of peace." The man declared that it was not by his will that the egg was cracked. He had not uncovered its fountain and had not laid hand upon it to break it; the blow that had struck it was by accident. With suchlike words did the man answer, seeking to atone for himself and his house; but the viper said: "Thou hast walked rebelliously with me; therefore will I hide my treasure from thee. I shall go and return to my nest, to the cockatrice's den, and thou wilt abide shamed and humbled, and wilt see me nevermore."

The parable: A man should keep afar from one who draws him near for the sake of his silver and his gold. When his welfare is entrusted to the hand of such, he will deal guilefully with him and deprive him of his soul for the sake of his silver and his wealth.

And I plied my poesy and said:

Him I thought a comrade, I discovered evil.
In goodly days and in bad season I tested him;
In days of joy and gladness I encountered him,
But on a day of stress in an evil season I lost him.

78

Ape & King

WHOSO JOINS COMPANY WITH
ONE OF FALSE LIPS, HIS SOUL IS
NOT PRECIOUS IN HIS SIGHT.

AN APE was exalted by a king. Many days he stood at his side, until he knew all his works, the food of his table, and the posture of his servants, how he exercised rule over them and maintained his strength. Nothing was concealed from him. The ape was eager to depart thence and rule over his brethren abroad. Came the day when he had prepared his flight, and he went forth into the field to his brethren, in the mountains of the wilderness and the forests in the clefts of the rocks. He said to the apes of the forest: "Woe to the land whose ruler is a child! Therefore are the good sunken low; every head is plucked bald and every shoulder sore chafed, and not one of you walls up the breach. Would that I were judge in the land, to render to the righteous according to his righteousness. No man would cheat his fellow; to each I would do according as he plotted, for I would ensnare the clever in their guile. Me it beseemeth to rule over my fellows and to govern them, for I am the son of sages, the son of the kings of the east." The apes hearkened to his words and said: "Thou shalt be lord over us." He chose the strongest and handsomest of the apes to be his guards, others to prepare his food, and the contemptible and weak-loined he made hewers of wood and drawers of water. The elders he established as judges. And it came to pass in the wheat harvest that two men went astray in the wilderness and came to the place where the apes had pitched their tents. They saw that there was a king within the camp and that everyone cried, "Long live our lord the king!" Before the king stood a small ape who found grace and favor in his eyes, wherefore the men thought him the king's son. At his right stood a concubine. By the thorny bushes they ate and drank and made merry. One was the chief of bakers, one chief of butlers, and one guarded the empty vessels. One was lightly esteemed and one, honored; one served and another was served, as is the law and statute among men, where the poor serve the powerful. The ape perceived the men and his reins were astonied. When he saw them he called them to himself with willing lips, and said to the greater: "I adjure thee, tell me what is in thy thoughts, whether the majesty of kingship rests upon me, whether my guardsmen are mighty heroes, whether my son be not exceedingly handsome, be he strong or weak, whether my wife who is joined to me is not comely to look upon, whether my attendants and they that keep my house and treasures are not exceedingly well favored." The man of good faith who had sworn to speak according to the sight of his eyes said: "I shall not belie my faith in all that I have seen. Like father, like son; like mother, like daughter; like manservant, like master; like maidservant, like mistress. Apes are ye and apes were your fathers;

blessed be he who made you despised. Thy wife is an ape, thy son an ape. The concubine who stands at thy right hand is of an aspect deformed and blear; all are vile and contemptible before all people. Ye are the most fractious and distorted of beasts, ejected from every communion of the living. Instead of honor ye have shame, instead of a girdle a rent, with plaguing thorns and prickling briar. After you no path is illumined, but ye make every lodging to stink. Your heritage is shame and disgrace." The king-ape watched the matter, and inquired of the second man, who said: "Would that I might live in thy environs! Happy are thy servants, and happy thy folk, who hear thy words and behold the beauty of thy suite, whose hand is exceedingly powerful. Thou art the handsomest of the sons of men; if all that are handsome were assembled at thy side they would not cause the light of thy countenance to dim. Thy wife is exceedingly well favored, the perfection of beauty and wisdom; at beholding her the heart of any king would exult. Beautiful of form is she, and beautiful of appearance. The majesty of thy son is beyond calculation; from the sole of his foot to the crown of his head he is without fault or blemish. There is no living thing his like for beauty." The apes applauded the liar and honored him without end. But the honest man's garments they tore, and they beat and bruised him. Then the king commanded that he be returned to his ways, to make his prowess known to the sons of men.

The parable is for a man in whose calculations there is no falsehood and upon whose lips no iniquity is to be found. If he join a company together with one of false lips his soul is not precious in his eyes, for the one distorts truth to utter flattery, while the other changes not nor alters. But if they are bound together by fetters of truth, in the end they will be honored. Woe worth the day when a man makes his soul filthy with his tongue, when he sweeps unrighteousness together to produce flattery. And because the lovers of flattery are many, the earth is defiled under its inhabitants.

79

Ape & Fox

ALAS FOR HIM THAT SAYS TO HIS
COMRADE, "THE BED IS SHORTER
THAN ONE CAN STRETCH HIMSELF ON."

AN APE saw a fox upon his way. The fox's tail was long and broad, so that it reached to the dust and he trod upon it with his feet. The ape followed his desires and implored the fox, saying: "Lo, I the ape love thee; give me a small fragment of thy tail. Tailless I issued from the womb, and my privy members are exposed. Thou hast more than enough for a covering, and the excess will make a portion. Or give it to my elder son, and he will pray for you and you will live long." Answered the fox in furious anger: "Enough of vexation and anger and deception! Thou askest of my tail, for the which thou hast not labored neither madest it grow. If I had double so much twice over, I would not give thee so much as to cover thy skirts, nor shall thy son exalt his glory with it. You shall be brought down to the ground, so that your foundation shall be uncovered."

The parable is for the doughty of heart who are far from righteousness. When they hear the cry of the needy not one says, "Here!" They respond not to the cry; and if they answer, their wrath is kindled, for their silver is precious in their sight. Their purse is broad but their heart narrow to show the needy compassion in their straits, and they look on when the righteous is forsaken. The hail shall sweep away the refuge of lies. Woe to him that says to his fellow: "The bed is shorter than that a man can stretch himself on it."

80

Woman, Husband, Knight, Vizier

LITTLE RECK THE LIVING
OF LOVERS NOW DECEASED.

A WOMAN smote her palms, and her eyeballs dropped tears; in bitterness of soul she sat forlorn, grieving in her heart for her husband who was dead and buried. In the wilderness beyond, a knight was hanged upon a tree, and the king's vizier and counselor went from city to city and cried out the king's decree that the body of any who took the hanged man down would be roasted in fire. Another knight, who strayed from the road, saw his brother hanging, and the matter vexed him sore, for he was his brother of the same father and mother. He made a way to his anger and at night took his own life in his hands and cut his brother's cords and buried him with his fathers. He feared mightily for his soul, lest they remove his head from upon him for that he had not kept the king's commandment. His flesh trembled for fear, and he ran to hide in the house of the woman who bewailed her husband in bitterness of soul. He spoke upon her heart with pleasant words, uttering goodly and comforting speech, and said: "To me shalt thou be for a portion, and I will betroth thee unto me in good faith. Forget thy sorrow and be comforted for thy husband, and come and lie with me."

And she, even she, said: "Thy fortune hath led thee true. The woman that hath now fallen to thy lot will answer thee in peace and open to thee." She pressed him to know all his affairs, and he told her what had befallen him: His soul was bowed down to earth, for upon that night he had violated the commandment of the king, wherefore he would die before his time and no more return to his kin. The woman said to him: "Be not afraid. My husband that is buried we shall hang in place of him that is hanged upon yonder tree, before a man can see to recognize his neighbor. Who shall know what we do in secret? There shall be neither speech nor words. Now heed my counsel; therefore hast thou come under the shadow of my roof." Quickly she led him to the grave, love making her line crooked, and they removed the buried man from his sepulture and did as they had said; she went and wandered in the wilderness to hang her husband that had been buried.

The parable: Few among the living take thought for those beloved and dear in their life. They pound their love to fine dust. He that dies can have no trust in those who embraced and kissed him. They put him from their hearts as one dead, and take no thought to remember his righteousness and keep his commandment—"Remember, pray, my loving-kindness, and deal not falsely with me nor my son nor my son's son." The man dies and they cover him with dust, and the living violate his commandment.

81

A Sick Man, His Daughter, a Physician

THEY THAT THINK TO ENSNARE
BY THEIR GUILE WILL FALL
IN THEIR OWN DEVICES.

A PHYSICIAN let blood for a patient and said to him: "This blood thou shalt watch over strictly until the third day, and upon the third day I shall see whether thou wilt go free of the disease that troubles thee and how thou mayest be relieved of it. By the blood I shall recognize every stumbling block, every plague and source of ill. All that plagues a patient is made manifest by the blood, whether it be green, black, white, or ruddy, for blood is the soul of all flesh." The patient bade his daughter to take the blood from him and guard it as the apple of her eye from being spilt hither or yon; for any that overturned the vessel, by man would his blood be shed. She took the blood and carried it away and put it underneath her chest. A cat walking by in innocence spilt the blood, whereupon her hands waxed weak and her spirit was darkened, and she said: "Alas, hope is perished! How can I say to my father, 'It is no more?' If he demand it, what answer can I give? May a lion rend him that spilt it; whether beast or man he shall not live." As her thoughts oppressed her, her reins counseled her to empty into the vessel so much of her own blood as the measure of what had been there. She bethought her of a leech and summoned him to her chamber and bade him drain her blood into the vessel. The physician came in his season to ascertain the source of the ailment, and the patient described his state. The physician asked for the blood which he had bidden him keep, and the patient replied that it had not been moved. The blood was sought, and the daughter brought it. When the physician saw the ruddiness of the blood and its aspect, it was accounted unto that man as an offense of blood. His wrath was kindled and he said in passion: "Thou art pregnant! Never has there been such a thing and never shall be, that an embryo be found in the body of a male. I do not wonder thou art sick; thy sins have caused these things. Thy guilt becometh such a man as thou; thou shalt put a knife to thy throat." The physician returned upon his way, and the patient sorrowed in his heart, for his heart misgave him. He summoned his daughter and again and again adjured her to know whether it was his blood she had brought without diminution just as she had received it, or whether she had spilt it on the ground and substituted other blood in its place; for that cause was his reason unsteady. The girl answered: "I did not spill the blood, nor do I know who spilt it. I found the vessel over-turned and all the blood spilt out of it; and lest thou fall angry with me, I substituted my blood for thine." Said he: "I thought thee a wall but thou art a door. From bran I hoped for fine flour. I thought thee shut-in, but thou art pregnant of a man, and of men hast thou sown seed. I had hoped for good and there came evil. Repeatedly I adjured thee in thy chambers not to go after young men. By the cords of thy guile hast thou stumbled; thou hast not clothed thee with beauty and majesty."

The parable is for those who think to trip others by their wiles so that they might suddenly smite them, but in the ambush in which they lurk they are caught by the guile they themselves contrived. Their evil and deception is revealed when their foot is caught in the snare they have hidden. He who plots to capture his fellow with false lines, false will be his return. So it befell the girl in her deception; her father thought her a virgin but learned that a man had

uncovered her source, and he despised the soul that had
been precious in his sight.

82
Ewe, Goat, Shepherd

GIVE EAR AND HEED: HE THAT DRAWS
THEE NIGH IS ACCOUNTED THY KIN.

A EWE was within the farmyard, and a goat, far from
its hedge. The shepherd waited for the ewe to yean,
and when she had yeaned he took the lamb and brought
it to the goat, who suckled it until it grew big and was
weaned; with much labor had she swaddled it. Then she
said: "Look to thy ways. Return to the land of thy
fathers and thy birthplace and do mightily. Thy mother is
a ewe, thy father a ram; if I have brought thee up until
now and swaddled thee and raised thee, thy father and thy
mother will rejoice when thou returnest unto thy people."
The sheep answered: "Nay, but thou art my mother, for
that thou hast heaped thy loving-kindness upon me. I shall
not call the ewe my mother, for she thrust me far from
her boundary and would see me no more; not to her is
my desire."

Give ear to the parable and hearken: He that brings
thee nigh is accounted thy kin; whereas he that keeps thee
afar, though he be thy kin, account him negligible in the
crowd. He is estranged from his brethren and an alien; he
troubleth his kin and is cruel. He troubleth himself who
says: "None may love me except he be of my mother's
and my father's kin, who gave me honor amongst the

dwellers of the world; 'tis a brother who is born for time
of trouble."

83

Thief & Witch

HEED NOT THE EVIL, WHO
STRENGTHEN THE HANDS
OF THE WICKED.

A THIEF brayed among the bushes, and thence plucked
mallows. In the evening, when the sun set, he could
go no further, desolate for need and hunger. Destruction
had wasted him at noonday; he was weary and toil-worn
and weak of hands, and he panted for thirst. A witch
came by upon that way and heard his cries for water.
She filled the waterskin with heaven's rain, and he was
humbled and confessed his transgressions. In his passion
he cursed his moments, for that he had ended his days
in shame and his sin had spread a snare for his footsteps:
"Woe is me for my mother that bare me; all that live
curse me for my transgressions and my sins. Mine iniqui-
ties have overtaken me." The witch gave him to drink
from the bottle, and rebuked him for that he had repented
of his evil. She hastened to approach him and hardened
her face and said to him: "Lo, I have found thee when
thou wert forlorn and heard thee when thou wert astray.
For thy manifold transgression thou didst curse thy days
and thy moments; therefore did I approach thee that thou
mightest not withold thy foot from evil. Nay, let thy
thoughts goad thee on, let thy feet run to do evil. Murder,
steal, commit adultery, pant after every work of deception; then will thy ways prosper, and I will bless them

150

that bless thee. Fear not of descending to the pit, be strong and of good courage, be not afraid nor dismayed. Even when thou art found tunneling through a wall, my hand shall give thee aid and my arm shall prevail over thee to afford thee escape from the snare with fire and magic and enchantment. Let thy foot hasten to deceit, and leave not thy former doings behind. At oppression and at famine thou shalt laugh, and I will walk in thy company. Give ear to the voice of thy handmaiden; add not nor diminish." The wicked thief yearned for evil, to resume his original practices; and he returned to his ancient uncleanness. His fury was ever vigilant to open its mouth for murder, but he did not remember to benefit his soul. He stole and slaughtered and sold. The helper he chose helped not, but counseled him to do evil. She taught him witchcraft and enchantments. Divination by arrows and consultation of teraphim were no mystery to him, and he spoke with her that was old in adulteries. Came a day when he went out into the field to lie in wait for merchants and plunder them. The nations heard of him, and he was taken in their pitfall. They searched out all that was closely hidden; one recognized his coat upon him and another said that he had killed his uncle. They overwhelmed his eyes and beat him with sticks, and they led him to a tree to hang him. He called to the witch: "Hasten to save me ere the evil cleave unto me. My enemy holds dominion over me, and I cannot escape. Spread thy wing over me; stand now with thine enchantments and with the multitude of thy sorceries." She answered him: "Until now I have helped thee and with my charms supported thee. I have compassed thee with pride as with a chain, in order to add drunkenness. So have I dealt with thee many times, but when I see that there are no bands to thy death, wherefore should I labor in vain? In an instant of time thou shalt be a ruin, and for this my counsel is vain and my right hand falls short. There shall come upon thee an evil whose dawning thou shalt not know."

The parable: Do not listen to the wicked, who strengthen the hands of evildoers, to wizards and sorcerers and magicians and dreamers, who say that evil shall not come nigh unto them and that they who work wickedness shall be built up. The hook of time is in their nose and its bridle upon their lips. Bloody and deceitful men shall not live out half their days, for with a single fall they are destroyed, whereas the righteous shall arise though they fall seven times.

84

Horse, Merchant, Man

HE WHO TRUSTS IN A MAN SHALL
NOT QUESTION OR TEST HIM.

A MERCHANT had a handsome horse. His neighbor visited him early, saying: "Sell me thy horse; take his value and put it in thy purse." The merchant answered him: "What matter the horse between me and thee? Mention his price no more; lo, he is thine without silver." The man answered: "Not so shall it be; he that hateth gifts shall live. Reveal his price to my ear and accept the money from me." Answered the merchant: "I would prefer to give him to you. But in truth I did not find this horse but bought him for twenty pieces of gold, and he is worth twice so much, not less than forty pieces of gold. If thou dost not wish him gratis, his sale shall be according to the evaluation of an arbiter. Let us both arise early to the vineyards, and the first man who encounters us shall judge between good and evil; thou shalt not add to his valuation nor diminish it." So they arose early in the morning, and a man came toward them on their path;

he had only one eye for his right eye was blinded. They said to him: "Let not thy palate sin. This horse hath been sold according to thy estimation; thou art the judge to determine its value, and the money of thy estimation shall be assured to him." Said he: "Far be it from me to belie my faith. The value of this horse I have examined in my heart, and I perceive that he is worth five pieces of gold. Yesterday I saw a horse like him sold for five pieces of gold; the shepherd and the farmer are witnesses." The merchant was angry and led his horse thence; his neighbor dropped five gold pieces from his purse, but the owner of the horse would not accept them. The man with goodwill brought the gold to his tent; mayhap he would persuade him and prevail upon him. Said he: "Give me the horse; here is his price." But the merchant made his palate rebellious. The purchaser complained to the judges, and the wise of heart were inclined in his favor. They bade him render the horse since the price had been fixed. The merchant took wily counsel, with deceit and guile and falsehood, and he told the judges such a story as this: If the man who had made the estimate had had two eyes, he would have made his evaluation twofold. But inasmuch as his right eye had been gouged out, when he inspected the horse he saw him with half vision and hence estimated him at half his value. Then said the judges: "Be thine that which is thine; discernment and understanding have fallen to thy lot, and thou art more righteous than we. With one eye he could not evaluate him."

The parable: Thus it befalls a man who puts his trust in humankind. Wherefore question and wherefore test him? When thou leanest upon him, he is broken; he speaketh with two hearts. So the merchant said to his neighbor: "Here is my horse, gratis"—and then wished to sell him at twice his value. Such a man taketh no delight in his honor. Thou mayest perceive here yet another proverb and parable: Enter not into judgment without a plan, but take counsel with thy thoughts ere thy lips speak. So did the merchant in his suit, when he brought his case into the light.

And I plied my poesy and said:

If thou bringest kindness out of my vessels,
Then canst thou draw kindness out of a rock.
A fool is he who thinks to fashion a nail of bad iron.

85

Lion, Wolf, Bear, Fox

WHO FORGES EVIL AGAINST
HIS NEIGHBOR, UPON HIM A
VAIN CURSE DESCENDS.

THE LION fell sick of the malady whereby he would die, and the wolf and the bear came to speak upon his heart, as did all the beasts of the earth after their kind. Only the fox hid himself, his heart panting to know the end of the matter, and what would follow the storm, and whether he would be missed by the king. He watched in secret to overhear what they would say, and he heard the wolf say to the lion: "My lord, hear my words. Send the fox to fetch balm of Gilead and spices and perfumes which will satisfy thy heart, for his is an ear that trieth words and his hand will grind the ointment. He is most expert of us all in paths and he knoweth the merchants of Gilead; there is none like him for wisdom and understanding." Said the king: "Summon him." But the wolf had acted with guile, to malign the fox, to bring him trouble and sorrow and keep him far from his ways. He spread evil reports against

him for not coming to visit the sick king and made false
rumors flourish. The fox heard his voice when he opened
his lips to spread destruction and said to the king: "The
fox is not here; may the whirlwind sweep him away, both
living and in his wrath." When he heard the words of
the wolf, the fox drew cunning from the depths of his
heart to inflict grief upon the wolf. Upon his lips a fire
smoldered to do unto him as he had plotted; he brooded
in his reins and sat silent until he saw the king's countenance furious. Runners issued forth posthaste to seek the
fox hither and yon, and the fox feared lest he stumble.
Slowly he came, leg touching leg and sole, sole as if he
were weary and fordone, and he said: "My lord the king
live forever! Hidden from him and unknown is the toil
and weariness I have undergone in seeking a healing remedy for thee. From the day upon which my lord fell ill
and lay him down, my rest ceased and my wandering began; until I reached Gilead and returned, I took no rest or
respite. These forty days have I been sated with vaga-
bondage, and the bread of my provision was dry and
moldy. I have passed over hills and valleys, mountains and
lowlands; in dusk and deep darkness I knew not where I
was. I have cut my life off like a weaver. But the physicians
gave me to eat of all the powders of the merchant, and all
with one mouth said they had chosen a remedy for thy
malady: Strip the skin of the living wolf from off his
flesh, and let the warm skin be taken for a turban for the
king's head, and it shall be for a sign and a wonder. All thy
loved ones shall come and sprinkle of his blood round
about thee. Say not, 'My hope is perished'; let them lay it
for a plaster upon the boil and thou shalt recover." The
king hesitated not to do according to these words. They
seized the wolf and flayed off his hide; only by the skin of
his teeth did he escape. He was a reproach to his neighbors, for they left him naked and his bones burned like a
hearth. The fox had caught him in his snare and had removed his hope like a tree. He stood opposite him, mock-

ing him and gnashing his teeth, and he said: "Art thou he whom the king delighteth to honor? Can the Ethiopian change his skin? Nay, but by the sayings of thy mouth hast thou stumbled, and by the wickedness thou hast forged against me. Upon thyself shall thy wickedness be poured, for I did dwell secure with thee."

The parable: He seeketh not peace for his soul who forgeth evil against his neighbor and speaketh against him in frowardness. When one letteth out water, it is the beginning of strife; his one verdict is death. Who slandereth his neighbor in secret, him will I cut off.

86

Hen & Mistress

YEARN NOT FOR THE DAINTIES
OF HIM THAT PERSUADES THEE
BY THE SMOOTHNESS OF HIS LIPS.

A HEN scattered her food and gathered it between her feet; she separated ears and cut them off; she opened her feet out to uncover the dust with her claw and the chaff blown out of the granary. Often she labored in vain, for she did not find enough to satisfy her. Her mistress looked upon her and saw that her heart was persuaded to give her soul livelihood by her toil; her mercies were warmed and she said to her: "Lo, I have swaddled thee and brought thee up, and therefore do I take pity upon thee for that thy corn is scattered and dispersed—the leavings of the hail—and thy soul falls short in seeking it. The seeds are rotten under their clods; therefore art thou

meager and wonderfully reduced—as one that gathereth
ears in the valley of Rephaim—and thou crouchest in a
troubled vale. Better for thee half a homer, aye, a homer
of wheat, as thou sittest at the gate of hope, than that thou

shouldst grieve all the day. Lo, I put before thee all my
grain, my threshing and the corn of my floor, worth a
hundred pieces of silver, current money with the merchant. Go not to glean in another field. Lo, thou hast uncovered the dust and covered it again; what hast thou
gathered this day, where is thy labor? Thou art wearied
but hast not found that for which thou hast toiled; before
thy bread cometh sighing." As the mistress spoke thus in
her ears, she was despised in her eyes, and she said to her:
"If thou wouldst give me each month thy granary full of
wheat threshed and ground, I would regard it as bread of
idleness. Better for me to endure poverty, to defile my
horn in the dust than that some cruel one drive me from
the granary. Whoso rests his hope upon another, the increase of his house shall depart. Better for me to go forth

free and seek whom my soul loveth and eat what I shall find; better for me to go forth and stray like a lost sheep. Sweet is the sleep of the toiler, and the ear which is innocent of man; but thou settest a print upon the heels of my feet. Let thine be thine and mine, mine, for that is my portion of all my toil. I shall go softly all my years in my toil, for I am no better than my fathers."

Hear and understand the parable: If a man say to thee, "Accept grain in place of straw," despise not what thine own hand findeth, for thou knowest not the weariness thou shalt find if thou hearkenest to his voice. Whoso despiseth the word shall be destroyed by it. Reckon the words of the enticers as nought; eat not the bread of him whose eye is evil. He that persuadeth thee by the smoothness of his lips, eat not of his dainties, for before thou are sated he will be sated with thee and on the morrow will thrust thee from his company. A violent man cajoles his neighbor and smites him with the rod of his lips. Even if he conclude a covenant with him he will cast brimstone upon his abode. The way of the scorners is to love scorn, and he that searcheth for good will seek favor.

87

Camel & Caravan

STRENGTHEN WEAK HANDS IF THOSE
HANDS ARE WEAKENED BY TOIL.

A CAMEL proceeding with a caravan knelt and lay down under his burden, and when he had no strength to rise all disdained him and hid their faces from him and made their eyes unseeing. He cried to them: "Hear me, my people! Surely I am your bone and your flesh, and your name is as my name; wherefore should riders and they that pass upon the road on foot say, 'This specimen shows their nature? When he is fallen and strayed from the path, the others go on.' See, there is no fault in all my toil. Be merciful unto me, be merciful, for ye are my brethren; until ye have raised me up, journey not forth. Do not, my brethren, do evil; lo, my heart is whole with you—how can ye ignore me?" They answered him: "If thy hands and feet put their strength forth to raise thee, then we shall surely help along with thee; but if thou cravenly follow idleness and lie inert as one fordone and weak of hands, then in vain wilt thou hope for our help, for that thou art sluggish in helping thyself."

The parable teaches and gives us to understand that weak hands incapable of help must be strengthened, if thou see a poor man whose hand falls short and he seeks thy face with a bitter and sorrowing soul, when his force is spent in vain and his hope and expectation have perished. But if thou see that poverty has prevailed over him by reason of idleness of hands and sluggishness, and his household are famished and impoverished by reason of idleness, then are all his comrades who hear his cry ashamed and his evil is revealed in the congregation, for he hath not made his hands firm, to gather as they did, and he begs of them with the brazenness of a harlot. This is the lesson of the vile and the nameless. And the sage who hath mounted the steps of good sense hath said: "I have tasted every bitterness, and there is no bitterness like the taste of begging."

88

Osprey & Pot

IF GOOD SENSE AND KNOWLEDGE
ARE IN THY REINS, THOU WILT
BRING THEM AND PLANT THEM
IN THE MOUNT OF THY HERITAGE.

THE OSPREY'S throat was dry with thirst and his
tongue failed for dryness, and he was wearied for
seeking rivers and broad marshes. For three days he went
in the wilderness and found no water, but on the fourth
he found a pot wherein was water. He knew not whether
it was half full or more, for the pot was deep and narrow.
The osprey would fain drink, but could not lower his head
to the water. His labor was vanquished, and the eagerness
of his soul redoubled. He descended to thrust the vessel
from its position and overturn it and spill its water. He
walked about it and pushed it, seeking to cast it down
with flank or shoulder, with beak or feet. When he saw
that he could not succeed, he gathered stones, mostly peb-
bles—for he that removeth stones shall be hurt therewith
—and his cunning devices taught him to cast them into
the pot. The waters rose up and reached all the brim of
the pot. And so he broke his thirst, and the cold water was
for a healing for his weary spirit.

The parable: Acquire wisdom and shrewdness and
clever schemes and cunning, for a man may be weak of
loins if shrewdness is bound fast to his heart. Better is wisdom than strength; therefore let knowledge and good
sense take root in thy thoughts. Thou shalt bring them
and plant them in the mountain of thy heritage, and sow

it with the seed of understanding, and water it from the fountain of sense. Turn not after folly lest thy soul be affrighted and polluted by it. And the sage hath said: "He that engages in wisdom shall not be put to shame if his neck be not stout and his body stalwart." He that takes my words to heart, the fortresses of the rocks are his stronghold. The wise shall see my parables and increase their wisdom; they will heed my sayings, for they are pleasant.

89

A Fearsome & Awesome Knight

BOAST NOT OF THY PRIDE, FOR THOU
KNOWEST NOT THY LATTER END.

THERE was a fearsome and awesome knight whose name was known in every city; a multitude of people trembled at his voice. To him princes were a jest. From afar he scented battle, and they feared to come nigh him, for the belt which was upon his loins and the shoe which was upon his foot. The thunder of the warlords and their horn blasts were for him a deliverance; when he heard the sound of their tramping, he put his hand forth to the top of the mulberry trees to shed the blood of the proud upon dry land. No archer put him to flight, for a brazen helmet was upon his head, and he dragged mighty heroes by his strength. At destruction and famine he laughed, at the lash of the whip and the rumble of wheels. His right hand was mighty to rend armor and crush it, as a thread is snapped on the weaver's beam. His hands fought for him, and the hooves of his horses were as flint. His name was bruited afar, for his rule was to pursue and overtake. When they that fought against him saw that the fir trees were shaken, they ascended the clouds and mounted the treetops. To a man they fled from before him, some in chariots and some on horseback. Dominion over the knights was placed upon his shoulder; they conferred upon him the glory of strength. If he encountered a merchant heavy with silver and gold, he made him the pottage which he loved. Against armed highwaymen too he put forth his hand, and overturned their glory to the earth. But while his honors were still fresh upon him, time put forth its hand against his peace and spread a snare for his footsteps. The days of the hero did not prosper. Whenever he entered battle he was either crushed or taken captive, and if he ran he stumbled in his going. There was no healing for his bruise, and his wound was grievous; his loins were filled with pain, his heart melted and his knees smote together. By a new name was he called: the weakling, not the hero. A bruised reed shall he not break. Every lowly man teased him with his hook; he had fallen from the height of his power. And it came to pass when he fell and rose not again, that his thighs were bound with chains, for one that dasheth in pieces came up against his face, and shut his eyes, and his hands were fettered from the bow, and those it had pierced gazed upon him. The merchant and the highwayman joined together; each was vigilant, and he retired from the place of their abode. Always he was in flight, and after him was a hue and cry, "Go up, thou bald one." If a price had been offered for his soul they would have removed his head from upon him. From that day forward he went backward, from before the flaming sword and the burnished spear. Instead of being stronger than his brethren and dominating them as heretofore, he went no more to battle nor took thought of it for any matter. Those who were his servants aforetime, he honored and served, and he was sated with disgrace instead of honor. Before the eyes of all his kindred he swore to burn all his gear of war and no more go forth to battle; and he kindled a great blaze wherein to cast his weapons. For he said: "I will burn and blot out prancing steed and leaping chariot, and with them corselet and helmet shall be erased; no shield or spear shall be seen." He thrust his sword into the belly of the horse he loved, and the haft also went in after the blade. Thereafter he broke the sword and did as he had said to his weapons. If hosts had feared them aforetime, there was not left of them any that survived or escaped. On the morrow he remembered his horn, upon which he was wont to blow in his woodlands and forests, and as he carried it to cast it into the fire, weeping as he went, his wife said to him: "Wherefore didst thou bethink thee of this to burn it? It is not a weapon of war; wherefore burn it in fire? Let thy heart forbear to destroy it; let it be a brand saved from the burning. Lo, I am ashamed of thy doing; be not as one dead." And it came to pass when his rib spake to him not once or twice, that he smote the rib with his staff two times and said to her in anger: "Thou art a daughter of rebelliousness; as speak one of the shameful women, speakest thou. The horn too was among my troublers, to rouse me to the sports of my youth. For when I heard the blast of the horn I ceased all my sighing and among the trumpets I said, Ha, ha! Therefore shall I cast it into the brazier. When I heard the horn's alarums I set my course thereby and roused me to war against mine enemies, and my sword came into play and seized them. And when I returned from battle I sounded my horn to hunt game and fetch it, and my dogs whetted their tongues, for it was the horn that mustered all the hosts."

The parable is to bear in mind this excellent law: He that scatters is like him that disperses; he that seizes a foot, like him that strips it. Even the horn, which was not a weapon of war, the knight verily sought to burn along with his weapons of war. If he that sees through his lattice turns a blind eye, his guilt is as the guilt of the thief.

90

Fly & Ox

A WEAK COMRADE LIKENS
HIMSELF TO HIS COMPANIONS
THOUGH THEY BE STRONG.

A FLY walking in the field saw an ox upon whose neck the farmer bound ropes and oxbows and bands and ceased not to ply his flanks with the goad. The ox set his face to plough, and the fly went and perched between his horns; as the ox traced the furrows, going and returning, the fly continued to sit upon his horn. His kinswoman the bee observed him and stood from afar to see what he sought between the horns of the ox and whether the ploughing would continue all the day. Said the bee: "Are the horns of the ox thine encampment? Why abidest thou among the sheepfolds?" The fly answered: "Know that all this field which is before us, I and the ox have ploughed by our strength. Do thou as we have done if thou hast the strength. Awake, awake, Deborah [bee]."

The parable is for the lowly who walks amongst the mighty or for the iniquitous who is mustered in the camp of the upright. In their counsel and in their strength he cannot stand, but by the utterance of his mouth he is joined with them to make his might equal to theirs and his wisdom to their wisdom. He says: "Thus have *we* done in *our* strength, and thus have *we* done in *our* wisdom."

91

Wolf & Fox

BETTER TO SOJOURN WITH THE
RICH THAN WITH ONE WHOSE
HANDS FALL SHORT.

THE WOLF said to the fox: "Hearken and I shall inform thee what thou shouldst do. Come with me,
and the king shall not know. I will teach thee what way
thou shouldst go, for the days of thy sojourn with the lion
have been long, and he hath oppressed thee and made thee
hunger, in order to prove thee. Lo, beyond the hedge I
have seen chicks, strayed from their mother and lost; thou
shalt come upon them suddenly and smite them. Seek not
their peace nor welfare. Breach the wall to the measure of
thy head; hasten and thou shalt find dainties for thy soul.
By the length of the hole and its breadth foxes may go
through it." Answered the fox: "If the lord of the house
and court is rich, nothing of all thou hast said shall be
wanting; but if he is poor and needy, my heart will es-
chew heeding thy counsel, lest he pursue after me and
overtake me and in the bitterness of his soul smite me to
death."

The parable: Understand what I teach thee, and be thy
heart not froward or rebellious; for if thou wax wise from
the parables of instruction thou wilt not be an example in
the assembly of the understanding. Better for thee to challenge the wealth of the rich than to challenge one whose
hands fall short, for the hand of the rich is abundant and
superfluous, and a sated soul despiseth honeycomb; if in
the morning they grieve at their loss, come evening they
sorrow no more, for their right hand is clothed in the

strength of the remnant that is escaped. But the poor are bitter of soul to purchase peace through war, for they have no escape or reserve. For their abundant passion and grief no violence can terrify or affright them; a lion's heart sprouts within them and gives them no respite, and they spoil the soul of those that spoiled them.

92

A Goring Ox & His Master

THE WICKEDNESS OF A PERVERSE
AND CROOKED MAN SHALL BE
HIS STUMBLING BLOCK.

AN OX sinned against his master. He was a gorer from yesterday and the day before; whensoever he took him out to plough he proved himself a goring ox. The master's hot anger rose against the ox, and he polled his horns with a knife and told his neighbor his demeanor was bad but that his long horns were cut off. And it came to pass in the morning, when he ploughed at his back, that the ox attacked him with his teeth. The master desired to debase all his pride and knocked most of his teeth from his mouth. And it came to pass when the grinders were gone from his mouth with only a paltry few remaining, the ox chased after every man, striking with flank and shoulder, nor was he humbled by his mishaps. Upon the third day he smote the master a great blow with his foot, and his neighbors said to him: "This outcome of his mutinous heart and deeds thou shalt not avail to remove from him by cutting off member after member but only by breaking him wholly."

The parable: Do not challenge a perverse man, for if thou ensnare him and bray him in a mortar, his perversity will not depart from him. Nay, keep him afar in every direction; he is an abomination that is not acceptable, for his heart is bitterroot and rank wormwood, the shoots of an alien vine.

93

The Man of the Field
Knoweth Hunting

THEIR HEARTS ARE IN DARKNESS

WHO BELIEVE IDLE TALK.

T HE MAN of the field knoweth hunting. He lurks for beasts and takes them, and they recognize him as he walks, by his bow and quiver. His spirit is watchful to hunt by night, wherein all the beasts of the forests stir; but ere he come they move away and their tracks are not known. Hart, roebuck, and hare, wild goat, pygarg, wild ox, and chamois, when they behold him face to face, all the hairs of their flesh bristle for fear of the oppressor they recognize. All these banded together for flight. A leopard under one of the bushes saw them all running with terror in their hearts and posted himself at the crossroads to learn what this might be and wherefore—whether for some dream or vision they had all fled as one. With one mouth they said to him: "Lo, we have seen the man lurking for us in the wilderness. His weapons of war are with him; his bow is firmly planted and always drawn for shooting, and his quiver is an open sepulchre. The arrows therein are his battalions, which his mighty arms scatter." Answered the leopard: "Move not from the camp; stand firm without turning." And when they turned their shoulder to go, the leopard did not stir from the battle line, and said: "I am not afraid of the man; if I meet him I will rend him in an instant and cut him off. His sure doom is death. Abide with me and fear not wrath nor cruelty; I will lead you as ye walk erect." The lurking man approached nearer for his shot; he trod his bow and shot his arrows to reach their target. Like lightning his dart issued forth and wounded the leopard in the second rib, so that his heart grieved and trembled. He gathered his strength for speedy flight and overtook the beasts for the soles of whose feet there was no rest. Before he neared them, they called to him: "Is it possible that the king should flee, with heart melted betake him to hasty flight? If thou hast not rent and slain the hunter, what price the assurance wherewith thou hast assured us?" Humbled by his anguish he answered them, and his voice was like a ghost's out of the earth: "Lo, my calculations were confounded. The man mine eyes did not behold, but at his bidding the fleas of death have bitten me; it is they that are called the sons of his quiver. Alas for the day that I trusted in my strength, alas for my breach and my aching wound! Such a hero as I am cannot prevail by great strength and prowess when he dispatches one of his tiny servants with me as its target, and the evil cleaves unto me and I die."

The parable: When thou seest men fleeing in terror, moaning and sighing with bitterness and breaking of loins, with every heart melted and every hand waxed weak before the whetted sword and the sound of the cries of the fordone, stand not in the place of evil if thou covetest thy life. Be not overpersuaded by thy strength or thy cunning, lest thy feet be plagued by thy devices.

94

Fox & Cat

WHO HATH IN HIM ONLY THE
PRAISE OF HIS OWN LIPS WILL
SWATHE HIM IN HIS SHAME AND
CLOTHE HIM IN HIS DISGRACE.

UNDER a tree planted upon waters the fox called to
the cat, saying: "Hear me; henceforward let us conclude a covenant, thou and I. My feet are swift as a hart's,
but thou art tried in mounting places where a fox may
not ascend. Lo, up above I have observed the flesh of a
sheep, moist and fat. If thou do not believe my words,
come and I will show thee that place. Under this tree shall
we eat it." The cat returned his answer: "At thy word
shall I march or halt." So they concluded a covenant between them, and both walked together. Said the fox to
the cat: "Open thine eyes and behold the place which is
before thee; see whether thou canst fetch the flesh. Ascend
thou on high and take thy captive, and I shall await thee
here until thou return to me in peace." The cat ascended
upward to the hanging flesh which he longed to eat; when
he reached the sheep he turned back carrying the flesh between his teeth. The fox, who awaited his coming, went
forward to meet him, rejoicing for that he had kept his
commandment, and uttered this counsel to the ear of the
cat: "Let us go under the tree and there make division by
lot, without guile or deception." As they walked together
along the road the fox pondered guile, plotting to seize
the flesh. As he approached nigh the cat, she scampered
hastily up a tree, before the fox, who was hungry and
impatient for food, could prevent her. The fox could not

climb the tree, and said: "Treacherous cat! Wilt thou eat whilst I stand in thy presence? Wilt thou not keep thy covenant and the utterance of thy lips? Give me wherewith to restore my famished soul, so that I grieve no more." The cat answered: "In the delight of my soul shall I eat flesh, and the belly of the wicked shall lack. I shall eat and thou shalt go hungry; the mocker shall be the mocked. Mine is this flesh, sound and fat, and the teeth of the wicked shall be set on edge." Said the fox: "Is this my requital from thee, is it thus thou dealest with me? For thine iniquity thou wilt be sore straitened, for I will besiege thee, to pay thee out measure for measure. What wilt thou do for the day of reckoning? Thy doom is graven and hewn. I will lay siege against thee with a mound and not stir hence until thou descend. Instead of the flesh I will take thy soul and remove thy head from upon thee." The cat answered: "This shall not be. I shall not die but live, for from the mountains are descending horsemen riding in pairs with spirited dogs before them. They are coming thy way; flee and find thee refuge, for wherefore should they smite thee to the life? Set thy footsteps upon the way before thou art delivered into their hand; attend to thy way, shake off futile dallying." The fox answered: "I am not afraid, nor am I terrified of the dogs. Who can reach me to harm me? My heart will not fail of its cunning and its hundred shifts and turns. Many such have I, wherewith to deliver my soul and elude their hands to go free. Nay, I shall not depart until I see thee caught in my snare. Between my teeth wilt thou be crushed; no more shalt thou chase after the rat." And it came to pass as he spake to him thus that the dogs came on in battle array and the riders tarred them on against him. One bit him in the back, one in the tail, one in the ears; one set his teeth in his neck, and one bit him in the sinews of his stones and testicles. When this mischief had befallen him the cat called out: "Do but work one of thy hundred shifts, and escape, so that thou wilt be master of thine own body; of what avail thy cunning if it save thee not in time of evil?"

The parable: This is the habit of boasters, the practice of sinful men who say, "Our hand is too lofty to put sickle to standing grain." They vaunt themselves much upon their cunning, and boast of their professions: "I am a weigher, I am a scribe; I am a smith, I am a tailor; I am a goldsmith, I am a merchant; I am a sage, and what other is there like me to equal me? I am a physician for every malady." But he delivers not his soul from his own trouble, nor does he sustain his household, for wisdom is not with him and there is no spirit in him. Who hath in him only the praise of his own lips will swathe himself in his shame and clothe himself in his disgrace.

95
Image & Man

A SOFT ANSWER TURNETH
AWAY WRATH AND LEADETH
NOT TO HATRED.

A GRAVER fashioned an image and finished it; by a craftsman was it made, and it was no god. A rich man sought eagerly to purchase it of the craftsman, for he wished to make it his god. Its beauty, its stature, its height, were correct in his eyes, and it was painted and portrayed with vermilion. Another man in the vicinity wished to purchase it to make of it a monument for the dead. He would set it up on good hewn stone, and therewith cover the grave of his kinsman whom he loved as his own life.

The image wept, and implored him that carved it to give him his body for his petition and his honor for his request; said he: "Lo, I am thine, and thou art my keeper; I am the clay and thou the potter, and in thy hand is all my spirit and glory, to exchange my honor for shame. Thy hands have made me and fashioned me; with compasses and a line hast thou drawn me, and wood that would not rot was chosen for me. For that I was precious in thy sight I have been honored. Thine was the workmanship of my pipes and tabrets, of my arms and my hands. Consider the end of such a beginning; have thou a desire to the work of thy hands. Deliver me not to the soul of mine enemies, who would vex me and purchase me of thee to cover the dead—a stinking and lifeless carcass—and so desecrate my manifest beauty. Would that my request come about, that thou sell me to one who will fear me and call upon my name! In my honor is thy honor, and the man who worships me will honor thee as he prays to me. My honor he shall not desecrate, and all they in the islands will show that they bow down to the work of thy hands. If thou take no delight in thy handiwork and its esteem, what profiteth the image which its fashioner hath carved?" Its fashioner heeded the image's petition, and sold it to the man who would serve and honor it.

The parable: Flatter any whose hand is strong upon thee; make thy counsel with him sweet, to draw his heart to thee; cajole the heart of the perverse, to gain peace, so that it may be good with thee and thy days may be lengthened. And one of the sages who saw visions of the Almighty hath said: "It is permissible to flatter the wicked in this world." And another sage hath revealed to mine ear: "Bow down to the fox in his day of power."

96

Conies & Hare

BETTER TO BE AT THE FEET
OF NOBLES THAN TO BE A KING
OVER FOOLS.

THE CONIES are not a strong people, neither fierce
nor deep of speech. They made their home in the
rocks, and the lion wrought havoc amongst them. Said
they: "Let us choose lords of our families; the rocks are a
shelter for the conies. If we place a king over us, what will
the lion do to us? Will he pursue after us in holes and in
caves, in rocks, in high places, and in pits?" They sent
messengers in all their boundaries to summon them all for
an appointed day. And they chose them a hare of tall
stature, old and strong and full of wisdom, and they said
to him: "We have chosen the king to rule and protect;
naught that issueth from thy lips shall be withheld. This
lion of whose voice thou art in dread, we know not what
hath befallen him. Ere he confound thee and become thine
enemy thou shalt shake his yoke off from thy neck." He
answered them: "Far be it from me to become your king;
I shall not rule over you, for there is no majesty of kingship nor glory nor dominion for one who ruleth over a
humble nation and a younger family. Very foolish is he
who seeks to hold sway over them; their judges are over-
thrown in stony places. Wherefore have ye angered me to
come up and walk in crooked paths? The kingdom and
the rule which ye would give me shall be the lowliest of
kingdoms. Better for me to be one of the least servants of
the lion than to rule over a people without strength or
power or might. My burden shall not rest upon you, but

we shall be fully equal." So he stayed them with his words and frustrated their plan.

The parable: It is better for thee to be at the feet of the nobles of the people than to be king and shepherd among vain folk. For amongst the great thou wilt acquire a name for thyself and in their company wilt thou be established and built up, whereas amongst the vile over whom thou wilt hold sway thou wilt become as one of them. Of old, great sages have said: "Be thou a tail to lions, but be not a head to foxes." And a sage summoned his son and said to him: "My son, my firstborn, thou art my might and the beginning of my strength. Know that the Rock hath ordained to exalt the humble and debase them that rise in pride, and dominion flees from any that seeks greatness. Therefore humble thyself, and thou wilt be raised on high."

And I plied my poesy and said:

If thy heart labors to pursue dominion,
Wonder not if what is pursued, flies.
Beloved, humble thy soul, and therein be exalted,
For grace and strength bloom for the meek.
The high of heart will not find honor; but know
It shineth upon the broken in spirit.
If thou choose greatness it will flee from thee
And liken thee to a budding boil.
If thou imitate the fox thou'lt be a lion;
Think thyself a lion and thou art bald.
If thou lovest to abide upright and perfect,
Thou shalt be a welcome guest in thy world.
In the measure that thou art humble and bowed down,
The majesty of honor will abound for thee.
Pride and haughtiness, keep afar; for its taste is evil,
Upon its path, a noisome stench.
Pride over all rulers beseemeth Him
Who ruleth over sun and moon.

174

97
Lion, Goats, Fox

FORGIVE HIM THAT HATH HARMED
THEE, AND GIVE TO HIM THAT
HATH DENIED THY REQUEST.

A LION sent his kindled wrath against goats, and hid the prey he had spoiled. The fox knew the paths of his house, and in his cunning silently stole in and ate of his flesh and gnawed of his bones, and was sated with them nor paid their price, as if he had found a windfall in the field and carried it off piece by piece. The lion perceived that the fox did not keep his faith but dealt treacherously, and he accosted him with soft words, not in anger: "This time it is bone of my bones and flesh of my flesh, which I have spoiled by my labor and the toil of my hands. My reins counsel me and my thoughts impel me to say, Go, leave my provision and eat thine own. If thy hand continue thus a second time I will teach thee 'Thou shalt not steal, thou shalt not covet.' The third time thou wilt sink as low as thou hast stood high in thy rebelliousness, and I will sweep thee out with the besom of destruction, nor will I forbear to break thy bones and rend thy sinews, as the weaver's cord is severed when he smelleth the fire. Shall the fox eat while the lion aches, and shall the lion's whelps not tread him down? If one that had spread his net for thee had fallen into thy hands, then only the slothful man roasteth not that which he took in hunting. But how did it enter thy spirit to search in my hidden store, and wherefore hast thou thus cheated me? Attend to my instruction, and return no more to folly." Answered the fox, sweetening his palate with persuasion: "Was I ever wont to do so unto thee? I have heard thine instruction and the sweetness of thine utterance; lo, I am insignificant; how shall I answer thee? Nay, I am ashamed and sorry for my deeds, and shall no more add unrighteousness to such as I have committed."

The parable is to deliver thee from the snare of the seducers. Have I not written thee excellent things—saws and proverbs and parables—that thou be hard to make angry and easy to appease? Nay, make thee paths in the heart of understanding, for yielding pacifieth great offenses. If thou see thy neighbor walking in the way of the violent and drawing his hand with the scorners, ceasing not to add to his sinfulness and kneading the dough until it be leavened, poured over with wicked things, then do thou rend the lock of his heart with pleasant speech and repeat thine instruction and repeat it again to turn him back—I know his pain—and say to him: "He that repeateth his folly and doeth a very horrible thing, his doom is one, mourning and lamentation. Who hath woe, who hath sorrow, who hath contentions?—Those who repeat their folly like you." If after the second admonition he transgresses, twice and yet again, then there is no hope for his latter end. Even the ox that gores is a proclaimed offender after three gorings. So is it graven upon the tablets: If he return neither knowledge nor understanding to his heart, thy hand shall be upon him first. And the sage hath said: "Forgive him that harmed thee, and give unto him that denied thy request."

98

Raven & Carcass

SILENCE ADDS, AND DIMINISHES
NOT, FOR A MAN OF KNOWLEDGE.

A RAVEN was over a river known to no vulture and
sailed by no galley. He flew hither and thither in his
hunger and was wearied of seeking his provision, until
evening. He came upon a place where he found a carcass,
and thereat rejoiced exceedingly. Out of the abundance of
his joy he gazed upon it and fluttered his wing and peeped.
His mouth he opened beyond measure and his voice was
heard afar. The ears of the eagle tingled, and he said: "I
will hasten to see whether it is the voice of them that
shout for battle or the voice of them that shout for being
overcome." He came to the raven and found him leaping
over the carcass and rending the flesh from the bones and
dividing it in pieces. The eagle raged against him in wrath
of spirit and smote him; there he established a statute and
ordinance for him and there he tried him. From that day
forward the raven raised not his voice to make his prey
known to the birds abroad.

The parable: Many have stumbled and been ensnared if
they were not silent when the season of their harvest fell.
Because they did not guard the opening of their mouth,
news of them reached the rulers and each roared like a
lion. All of them shall be as thorns thrust away, lurking in
hiding like a lion, and they bring an evil name upon them
until no gleanings are left. Gleefully they seek them that
stumble, to get them provision and plunder; the extor-
tioner is at an end; the spoiler ceaseth. By the utterance of
the mouth and want of silence hath the spirit of men been

cloven. And I said to him the utterance of whose lips is not guarded and restrained that he is a cake not turned. And the Preacher who hath sown understanding hath said: "The wicked is snared by the transgression of his lips." And the Arab hath said in his instruction to his firstborn son: "Thy secret is thy captive; if thou reveal it thou wilt be its captive."

And I plied my poesy and said:

Who stumbleth with foot, little is his stumbling;
Who stumbleth with mouth, loseth his head.
Know that whoso guards his mouth and tongue
Guards his soul from trouble.

99

Fox, Wagon, Fish

HE THAT IS FILLED WITH DECEIT
AND FALSEHOOD INCREASETH HATRED.

A FOX went upon his way traversing the earth in its length and its breadth, and he turned his face hither and yon, and lo, a wagon came upon his way, filled with fish from the sea. He craved them for the delight of his soul and bethought him of a trick to work; and for the longing of his soul he worked it. He made himself as one dead upon the road, though he was sound of body. He spread his palms upward, so that he seemed as one whose knee had stumbled in the wilderness and who had fallen at the crossroads and was lying dead in the roadway. The wagon driver lifted his eyes and saw before him the fox, who had knelt and lain him down and was stretched out as if anguish had come upon him. He lifted him and carried him (the fox rose not nor stirred) and put him in a bag and covered him, for he feared lest his pursuers should recognize him. He hid him under his skirts, lest the inquirer see him, and covered him with garments until he grew warm, and he lay with the fish in the wagon. Them the fox consumed utterly, and he filled his belly with them; his soul took no mercy upon them. When he separated a part and ate it he said in his heart, "Shall I eat and leave behind?—I shall not rest until I engulf all, even the full vessel that is set aside." So he ate of the fish and was sated, taking as many as seven in his mouth, for his satiety ran over. Then he dug through the bag and alighted from the wagon and ran away and entered a stronghold he found and hid him with the prey yet between his teeth. The wagon passed before his face without the driver perceiving that the fox had fled. Quietly the fox went on and stood in a path in the vineyards, for he feared them that might rise against him; his footsteps stirred not, nor was his hiding place discovered.

Now as he remained there hidden, in fear and in dread and in terror, there entered the place a wolf, weary and fordone and sorrowful, for that his soul panted for prey. The wolf lifted his head and came forward to meet the fox and greeted him, and the fox responded in due form, but bethought him of devices to remove the wolf from his boundary, for he feared him, lest he come and seize that which was his. The wolf inquired after his peace and asked what it was he carried in his mouth. The fox answered in a clear voice, with guile and frowardness and deception: "Peace have I and peaceful be thy coming; greatly have I rejoiced at thy speech. Lo, I went forth to yonder water and found it congealed with cold. Upon it I walked, like a strong man that runneth a course; in the ice I made a hole, and in the hole placed my tail for the space of an hour. Around my tail came the fish, and formed a crown about it as if held with fishhooks. I seized them as with a net and made them my provision, whereof I have eaten and am satisfied. Go thou then and do as I have done. I know thou hast labored in vain; I believe thou hast found nought. To restore thy weary soul eat but one fish and it shall refresh thee." The wolf longed for like dainties, but bade the fox farewell and blessed him and said to him: "Be thine that which is thine; I will not trust thee, to thrust my tail into holes, lest the accursed and bitter waters come upon me." The wolf ran to the pool, which was all frozen with the cold of the night. There he observed a hole made by the shepherds to water their flocks at midday, and he said in his heart: "For all my innocence I have sinned grievously in suspecting the fox. Yet hath he not put his hand forth for deceit, but the truth is established in his mouth, and his hands have acted in good faith. I see the pool and the hole in its surface." So he thrust his tail in the hole and sat by to await the hour when the fish would be gathered in his snare. The sun passed over and was gone and the cold waxed stronger, until the tail was frozen in the pool. But the wolf was filled with joy, for he imagined that he was catching fish with his tail. Said he: "My tail is exceedingly heavy; I know that my seat is strong. Better is this than gain of silver, if all the fish of the pool be gathered. Now shall I be the diligent one that profiteth. But I am fearful of the sons of strangers, lest they see me and slay me and turn me back empty." Then the wolf collected his strength to arise from his place, but could not, for the cold had fallen upon his bottom. His tail, which was in straits, pained him sore; and he cried a great and bitter cry, for that he could not rise to his feet, for the joints of his ankles gave way. The shepherds heard his voice and were astonished, and they went to see what had befallen him. They sought their dogs to urge against him, each man tarring his own dog on, and the dogs attacked and bit him. They surrounded him on all sides, while he perforce remained fixed, and they smote and pounded him to desolation. In the anguish of his spirit he took courage; but his force was spent in vain, for his tail was held fast in the ice. The sun shone upon him, and the shepherds multiplied their blows. They embittered his life; the archers hated him and shot their arrows at him, and discharged upon him every missile that wounds, for he was their enemy from of old. Said they, "Come and let us destroy him." Because he had not guarded his way the shepherds dealt violently with him; all shouted against him, nor were they afraid to come nigh him. With the passion of his strength he persisted in his choler, though his eye was dimmed and his moisture desiccated, until the ice was broken. In their company then he did not tarry, but ran to the forest in a windy storm. Even there he found no respite, for the strong-spirited dogs ever clove close to him. Loudly men called: "Pursue him speedily, and ye will overtake him"; and the dogs gave voice and barked at him. He escaped from his pursuers, for the forest wearied them so that they returned from pursuing after him; to enter the forest they were loath. The wolf hid under a bush, beaten and bruised and subdued; all alone he grieved, and found no helpmeet to console him. And he said: "Surely the bitterness of death is passed. The fox made my way crooked and thought to kill me; I was foolish to believe him when he guilefully bade me seek prey in the pool."

The parable is for a man filled with deception and falsehood. He plots hatred against his neighbor and makes of himself an ambush; he conceals a gin upon his path and rejoices at his great cheat. Woe to the rogue, woe to his neighbor! Ever doth he seek an occasion against him. Upon his lips there is no truth; his ears he maketh heavy and his eyes, blind. Out of the wicked issueth wickedness; against his neighbors he speaketh iniquity. Hatred maketh the line crooked.

And I plied my poesy and said:

I that speak am innocent of deception, pure and
    guiltless;
Pure be he who beareth the mien of one that kisseth.
He that compoundeth iniquity is as chaff within
    grain;
Lips of grace make strong the heart of the pure and
    blameless.

IOO

Demon & Ship

THEY THAT INSTIGATE QUARRELS
DESTROY STRENGTH AND MIGHT.

THE DEMON walked in company with his mother
over a large expanse, going to and fro in the earth
and walking up and down in it, until they came to the
shore of the sea, where they lifted their eyes and saw a
ship filled with horses and men. The ship was on the point
of foundering, for the sea and its waves stormed and
roared. The passengers cast all the vessels in the ship into
the waves to lighten it; their flesh trembled for fear of the
sea. One called to another and bade him cast into the sea
his adornment and all that his eye coveted and to confess
his transgressions and his rebelliousness; then did they
empty all their precious things from their bags. The
sailors too were affrighted and cried out, and every man
shook his treasures from out of his bosom, for the storm
waxed greater. Said the demon to his mother: "If thou
hadst been with them this day they would have said that
by thy hand had this befallen them. So have they done
many times over; they utter slander against thee when the
day of turmoil and confusion comes upon them, though

thou hast committed no violence nor deception." The mother made her reply forthright; she hardened her face and said to him: "Though I be not there, many have I found among those I have raised and swaddled and made great who are willing agents to do my desires. From my hand hath this befallen them; they will lie down in sorrow. Upon earth men shall fear my deeds, for from me issue destroyers and desolators."

The parable is for those who instigate quarrels, for slanderers and maligners. Of their tongue's wrath they sow seed among the wise; their hearts and their lips are eager to do evil. They prophesy false burdens and causes of banishment. Each of them intrigues against his neighbor. They make kings rejoice by their evil, and princes, by their falsehoods; and when their slander succeeds they boast in the midst of their congregation and declare that their agent slander hath done prosperously. But the sage hath said in his wisdom that a man's agent is accounted as himself.

101

Merchant, Robbers, Knight

THE TREASURERS AND JUDGES
ARE FLED AND WANDERED AWAY;
NEW ONES FROM NEARBY HAVE COME.

A MERCHANT walked in company with wicked men. And it came to pass at midday, when they entered a forest, that they observed his clothing was desirable. The men of deception hastened upon him and, like emptiers, emptied him out wholly, and smote him and spoiled him and bruised him, so that he was left stunned and confounded, plagued and bruised and battered. With the string of their bow was he bound and tied. Naked he went forth, without a garment; he wished to go and heal himself of his wounds, but had no strength and fell to the ground and spilled his blood upon earth's bosom. There was none to help him. The flies gathered upon his flanks and arms and encamped round about all his wounds, to pluck and lick the blood from his gashes, like a swarm of sucking bees. They ate and were abundantly satisfied, and because of their satiety rested there and remained. Now a knight was riding by that way, and he turned and saw a man lying with his hands tied behind his back, likely to be consumed in a day, for all his body was bare and insects after their kind lodged upon it, and his belly was lying in the dust. The knight had pity and dismounted from his horse and cut the man's bonds. With branches and leaves from the forest he brushed the insects away and made them

all flee, until none was left and the body of the wounded man was exposed. The man cursed the knight with a mighty curse, reproaching and reviling him with a voice like a ghost's issuing out of the earth. He said to him: "Why hast thou chased the flies away? May he that troubled me trouble thee. Wherefore hast thou troubled me? What have I done to thee and how have I vexed thee? Surely out of the wicked cometh forth wickedness. I am mortally wounded, though I have not transgressed; lurkers have surrounded and set upon me, and have beaten and battered and bruised me. Woe and lamentation have they that plundered me inflicted upon me; they took my veil from upon me. And now hast thou arisen after them to bring anguish to my heart, for thou hast added pangs to my pangs." The knight answered: "Nay, but from thine afflictions have I redeemed thee. What have I done to thee and how have I vexed thee that thou slanderest me like a fool? Did I fear the great multitude that was destroying thy body and cutting it off? Thy soul was brought nigh to the pit and thy life to the slayers. Them that were upon thy naked flesh I cast down to waste and desert ground and removed their burden from upon thy shoulders, so that thou wilt nevermore see them and no more be pained. Wherefore hast thou repaid evil for good, and for my blessing a curse, and for my benefaction destruction?" But the merchant answered the knight with harsh words and said to him: "He that exacteth vengeance shall never remain silent. Thou hast scornfully entreated me and with thine outstretched arm troubled me when thy hand chased from upon me the flies who were already sated with my blood. My body they covered like a garment, but after thou hast put them to flight strangers will come and draw my blood and afford my sinews no rest. Better for me to endure fly and wasp that have eaten to satiety and drunk to drunkenness than to endure those not yet sated. Therefore are my words harsh."

The parable is for treasurers and bailiffs which the folk change and replace when they have emptied our purses of

silver. Those men are at peace with us, for we have sated
their bellies with dainties and filled their purses and their
cups to overflowing; with our silver has their anger been
muzzled. But in their place they have installed others, who
are not wearied with robbery—new men that come from
anigh—wherefore they draw as the lodestone draweth.
The young lions do lack, and suffer hunger, and turn
them toward gain. The principal folk they judge with
bribes, they deny knowledge of their acquaintances; they
leave a man no livelihood, no man is free under their
power, and they transmit their commandments to a second and also to a third. Therefore give ear to my saying
and bear away my counsel: Dismiss not the old judge from
before the new. Time prevaileth over a man who hath
dealt harshly with his neighbor twice or thrice. Therefore
should a man during the span of his life love the judges
whom he already knoweth, for the new shall receive of
you his standing. Be thou vigilant to aid in his rule that he
be not removed from the city.

102

Camel & Mountain Goat

WHOSO IS NOT SATISFIED WITH
WHAT SUFFICES HIM WILL LOSE
EVEN HIS DAILY BREAD.

BACK of the desert a camel saw mountain goats. Their
young ones were in good liking; they grew up with
corn. By their side lay he-goats with horns upon their
heads; there all the beasts of the field disported themselves.
The camel entered the camp and came nigh a goat with

horns. He vaunted himself upon his form and image, upon his strength and lofty stature, and that all that walked on fours before him were as grasshoppers in his sight. Answered the goat: "Verily thou art desirable and pleasant, and if thou but hadst horns like mine thou wouldst be very strong." These words the camel took to his heart, and he went to the master who ruled over him and said: "Though size and strength have fallen to my lot, all this profiteth me naught when I see animals with horns upon their heads. Though my little finger is thicker than their loins, they gore west and north and south and malign my tallness of stature and let their bridle loose before me, saying they would gore even me. And now, my lord, hearken to my voice. Cut me mine ears off, and make thy latter kindness loftier than thy first: Give me horns for my forehead." And he importuned him sore. Said his master to him: "Wilt thou then constrain me? Wherefore hast thou made thine asking stubborn? Better hadst thou kept silent in thy petition." His master dealt bitterly with the camel and cut his ears off to their midpoint; he turned not back his hand, nor did he show pity. Therefore hath the camel small ears.

The parable is for one who has sufficient for his needs yet asks for more than his regular provision and says to his neighbors that he cannot live with what is in his hand. His root shall be like chaff and his bloom ascend like dust. In an instant his wealth will be consumed, for at the appointed time a sword is whetted like a razor to destroy and extinguish what greatness he has remaining. And I have found in the book of memorable wisdom, "Greed is partner to blindness." And the Preacher hath written in the proverbs of his wisdom [Proverbs 25.16]: "Hast thou found honey? Eat so much as is sufficient for thee, lest thou be filled therewith and vomit it."

And I plied my poesy and said:

When the camel asked for horns they cut his ears off;
Thus ever doth it befall the greedy if he possess wealth
and flocks.

103

A Man Ploughing His Tilth

BETTER TO SEEK AND SEARCH
IN ONE'S HEART WHO IT WAS
THAT HATH PASSED HIS GOODNESS
BY HIS FACE.

A MAN was ploughing his tilth and with his mattock
cleaving the earth and crumbling it, when he found
a hoard of precious stones, gold, and silver. Thereupon
did he burn incense to his drag and sacrifice to his net; and
of the sheep and oxen which were with him he offered
holocausts to that place. He honored it with all his might,
and he called to his people to do honor to the place. "Do
ye as I do," quoth he. "Him that sacrificeth a thank offer-
ing will I honor; all of my days will I honor him with my
praise. Verily, I am rich; I have acquired strength for myself." No more did he plough or sow or reap, no more
stitch together or rip, no more cast manure upon the furrows of the field; his yoke was taken off for fatness. But
he kissed that place and honored it with his praises. And
lo, the voice of fortune spake unto him: "What doest thou
here that thou bowest down and worshipest thy land? Is
thy reverence not thy confidence in the store of silver
which thou lovest, in the hewn pits which thou hast not
digged? Me hast thou not remembered in thy thoughts,
though I caused the treasure to fall in thy way. Therefore

will I return and take from thee my gold and my silver, and in their place I shall awaken mine anger against thee. No longer shalt thou honor the earth with thy praises, with my gold and my silver which I have given thee. From that day hast thou lifted thy head and bestowed thy silver upon all that thy heart desired. I shall no longer take mercy upon thee; in the sweat of thy brow shalt thou eat bread, until thou return to earth. Naked camest thou forth from thy mother's womb, and naked wilt thou return thither. The pride which hath burgeoned in thy heart is a bud that yields no meal." And he let him go, and so it befell him; when he came to count the treasure and set it in order, though he had but just come forth, he sought but found it not. And he returned him to his station as it had been aforetime, to the ploughs and coulters, the forks and the axes, to reap his harvest and plough his tilth, and his soul was humbled with toil.

The parable teaches a man to search and seek out in his heart who it was that passed his goodness before his face, to requite him according to his beneficence and to praise him according to his deserts, to fulfill his request and do his petition. Let him not change or supplant him, to praise another in his place; but him shall he honor and his people. His mouth nor hand shall fall short for him, as befell the man of the treasure trove, who had honored not him that had exalted his honor and his majesty, but embraced and kissed him that did him no honor.

104

The Ape, His Two Sons, a Leopard

THOUGH A MAN DIFFERENTIATE
BETWEEN TWO SONS, IN THE END
THE DIVERSE WILL BE MINGLED.

UPON a rock near a bush were an ape and his two sons, of whom he loved the younger and hated the elder. When a watchful leopard descended from his lair the ape trembled for himself and the son he loved, for he saw that he was come from the mountains of the leopards. In great fury the leopard came on to destroy and lay waste; he roared over his prey and made a way for his anger. Said the ape: "Of him that I hate I shall know how to be bereft; I shall hide my face from him and he shall be for devouring." And he took him and cast him over his back, intending to present him to the leopard first. But the younger, upon whom he took pity, he carried between his legs as he ran. When he saw that the leopard was approaching nearer he wished to hurl the ape upon his back to the ground, but that one perceived his willfulness and in his desire to deliver his soul grasped hold of the fringes of his hair. When the ape saw that he could not throw him down and the leopard was drawing very nigh, he forsook the one he loved and himself escaped with the one that held sway over his back. When the ape saw that his scheme was frustrated, his reins and heart clove to the one he hated, and his hatred was turned into love; he took pity upon him as a man takes pity upon the son that serves him.

The parable: A man should love his sons in equal measure, for him that he loves best and in whom he reposes his

hope the wheel will suddenly ravish away; shut thine eye
upon him and he is gone. But him that he hated and kept
afar will restore his soul and sustain his old age.

105

Boar, Lion, Fox

WHO MAKETH HIS HEART HARD
FOR AN OCCASION, ALWAYS IT
WILL BE ILL FOR HIM.

A BOAR came and went as was his way in the court of
King Lion. The lion said to him: "What business
hast thou near me? Come no more into my boundary and
render not the habitation I take delight in unclean." The
boar answered him: "My lord, I have heard." And it came
to pass in the morning and lo, the boar walked round
about the lion's lair, and the lion waxed angry and cut off
one of his ears. He called to the fox and said to him in the
boar's presence: "If this swine shall not depart from me,
show him no mercy and no compassion. This boar out of
the wood doth waste my lair, which is my shelter from
tempest and stormwind. His is a strange work; now hold
him not innocent but slay him." But the boar made his
heart hard and his neck stiff, and the lion in his furious
wrath cut both his ears from his head and pierced his eyes.
But the boar still enraged him with the turds of his dung
and made the surroundings of his lair unclean, wherefore
the lion said to the fox: "Attack and slay him; his head
and knees and entrails, the goodly portions of shoulder
and thigh, put thou in my way upon the road." The fox
butchered the boar and separated his parts. But when he

saw that the heart was fat he took it to see what might become of it; he could not refrain him but ate it. All of the members he arranged in order. The lion came to see the pieces of the boar and observed that not one was withheld; of all the bones not one was broken; he found them all in a row, the head and the fat. But when he came to the entrails, he did not find the heart, and said to the fox in anger: "How didst thou deal deceitfully with thy lord? Where is the heart of the boar which thou didst wound? How couldst thou desire to conceal it from me? And now I shall requite thee according to thy deed; as thou hast done so shall it be done unto thee." The fox answered in his wisdom: "My lord, not against me falls this complaint. Incline thine ear to my saying: Herein art thou not right, and I shall refute thee. Thou didst perceive the boar's rebelliousness and discern his folly; there was no heart within him. When I arranged his members before me, I sought it but found it not. Therefore was he not instructed by the words of the king. It was for want of heart that the fool walked according to his folly, and for want of heart thou didst take his ears and eyes when he hardened his face against thy commandments. My lord the king is wise and will walk in uprightness; he will not frame an accusation against his servant." The lion answered: "I have heard thy voice. If thou be wise thou shalt be wise for thyself. Thou art more righteous than I, therefore shalt thou sit at my right hand all my days. There is none so wise as thou; I will call thy name 'My delight.' Thou shalt be over my house, and according to thy word shall all my people be ruled."

The parable: If thine inclination constrain thee to commit an impropriety, seek among the roots of thine imaginings to deliver thee like a man armed. Envy not men whose hearts and ears are uncircumcised; from what time they went forth from Egypt have they been uncircumcised. A man whose heart and ear are uncircumcised, his evil thoughts are fringes which prevent circumcision. But look thou to a way by which thou mayest go forth from thy sins to enlargement; then wilt thou establish thy soul that it may live. Wisdom giveth its possessors life and provideth healing for great sinners. And I have found in the book of the princes: "Kings judge the earth; the wise judge kings."

106

The Lion & His Son

IT IS GOOD TO BEWARE OF THE
WICKED IN EVERY WAY, FOR SONS
DO THE DEEDS OF THEIR FATHERS.

THE LION, who is king of the beasts, dwelt in the habitations of lions and followed the usages of his people; with the peril of his life he got his bread, as his fathers had done. He tore in pieces enough for his cubs and strangled for his lionesses. Now when he fell mortally sick and his own soul abhorred him he called to his firstborn son, who was in his city ruling over all that was his, and the young lion responded to his voice. He called to him "My son"; and he said, "Lo, here am I," and he knelt and bowed down before him. He commanded him and said to him: "My son, keep the commandment and live. Govern thy sheep and be thou strong and soldierly. Lamb and ram shall be for treading under the sole of thy foot when thou art yet young and tender; when thy strength waxes great thy hand and spirit shall not fall short. Thou shalt crouch and lie down like a young lion to seize prey and overtake it. Thy foot shall be fleeter than theirs. To the

193

young of kine and to ass colts thou shalt leave no rest, for thou shalt pounce upon them in anger according to thy pleasure. From thy lair thou shalt go up like a lion, and all that rebel against thy lips shall not live. Thou wilt then be king over all that walk on fours. Over the sending forth of the feet of the ox and the ass thou shalt rejoice and over the keeping of all cattle; their outgoing shall be at the setting of the sun. Always for food shall they be, not for merchandise, only for the possession of a heritage. And when thou goest down and reclinest at thine ease, be not wanting in prudence. Of all the beasts and cattle the clean is forbidden thee, but with the hare and the coney thou shalt laugh at destruction and famine. Neither from the swine shalt thou abstain, for its flesh is fat. Thou shalt answer and say Amen. Nothing shall be wanting to thee, but thou shalt eat flesh to thy heart's desire. From all cattle shalt thou draw it forth with a high hand, and over all beasts thy hand shall prevail and thou shalt destroy their majesty.

But of the sons of man beware, for his devices are many. He will ensnare thee in his gins. Though thou be stronger than he, in craft thou canst not evade him, for he arms his hand with a bow as with a grate network to put thy foot in the stocks. For him a precious cornerstone is the pit and the snare and fear, and thou wilt descend to the abyss of destruction. Thou wilt not prevail against him, for none upon dust is his like. Who indeed is his equal? All cattle, every one, are slaves to man, both horses and mules; he desires them for his seat and harnesses them to his chariot. Day after day he lays his burdens upon asses; he ploughs with oxen and slaughters them for food. He is strong in the shearing of sheep. The souls of ox and lion and sheep sorrow, and the lamb is led to the slaughter. Therefore do I bid thee hearken to my counsel and keep my commandment, lest after my death thou be destroyed if thou violate words of truth. Lo, I shall die, as is the way of all the earth, and thou wilt break forth this breach upon thee. Be not afraid, neither be thou dismayed. But guard thy soul that thou go not down to the pit. Be thou strong and of good courage."

Thereafter the king commanded that his son be seated upon his throne in the sight of all his officers, that so they might be among his helpers. And after he had given his commandments he fell upon him and kissed him, and after he had spoken his spirit departed and his eye was dimmed and his moisture fled and his heart was poured out and his majesty was turned to destruction and he was gathered in to his people. The son's mercies waxed warm and he cried out: "My father, my father—thou that didst hold sway over ram and hart—majesty of royalty, chief of battle hosts, woe unto us, woe, that thou art enclosed in desolate land." And he lifted his voice and wept over him and kissed him. At his sound his family trembled and all his ministers with him, and all came to lament the king: "Alas for our lord, alas for his majesty! If the boldness of his face be changed, what shall his orphan children do? After him we shall grope like men blind; wherefore is his chariot so long in coming? He hath fled into concealment. Wherefore hath our shade departed from us? Would that he even hate us and return upon us all the evil that we wrought him. Woe is us that we have sinned; we are perished, lost are we all if our king who was celebrated among the nations hath fallen." And the peoples lamented him, but the son would not be comforted. He enjoined a mourning of seven days, and when the mourning passed, when the strength of the burden-bearer was decayed, and his place knew him no more, they took the dead up and buried him in the rock of his lofty mansion. They called its name High Place, for it was to be a monument whence to behold the carcass of the lion. And it came to pass after they had buried their glory and their treasure that the people turned and departed. And they brought the king's son back and comforted him in his house, and gave their pledge that they would love and serve him.

And when the king returned to his house, he sat upon his throne according to law and statute, and the kingdom prospered in his hand. He turned hither and yon in his roaring, and no beast could stand before him; all were unstrung and confounded at his rebuke. And when the heart of the king was glad in his joy, and his spirit was greatly exalted, he opened his hands wide and made a banquet for all his servants; the drinking was according to the law, none did compel. They raised an ensign to the mountains to satisfy every living creature with favor, with the butter of kine and the milk of sheep. They covered their face with fat until their hearts were appeased toward their king. During the days of the banquet the king called to his ministers and enjoined the chiefs of his soldiery to make the young men rejoice and give the stalwarts confidence, to make them officers over the host, captains of thousands and captains of hundreds. All gathered together and formed a united band—bears and leopards, lions and swine, horses and elephants, dromedaries and camels; the foxes hastened to join the assembly, and there were unicorns and monkeys by thousands of thousands, until there was no place to stand. The camp was exceedingly heavy, and the king was eager to behold it. He made a pavilion there and called to his ministers and household and said to them: "Choose ye out the heroes that ye see before me to be officers in the host and devastate city and province." And they did according to the words of the king; they made the leopards generals and the bears lieutenants and the wolves prefects to fight against the dogs. The deer were runners, and the foxes counselors, for these were clever when they emerged naked from their mother's womb. They arose with a high hand and rejoiced and sang and made their voices heard, crying "Long live our lord the king!" And the people saw and shouted and fell upon their faces, and the king rejoiced over them. To his tent then went each man from the treasure-house, for in the month of spring he had opened his father's stores and multiplied his gifts and made presents to all that came thither, and blessed them, and they went in peace. The people went upon its way, and the king remained in his pavilion with the flowers of his family who made his kingdom strong.

And he went to his stores and brought forth all the treasure of his fathers; but when he saw that what had been hidden away was reduced, he couched in his den and said: "I will clothe me in strength and pass through the wilderness and awaken all my wrath upon any that encounter me. I will avenge me upon mine enemies and fill my lairs with prey. And if I encounter man—though my father bade me beware of him, for that his eyes shine bright and he sees from afar, oppresses him that is beneath him and envies him that is above—may he so do unto me and more also, I shall transgress my father's commandment. As the man is, so is his strength; if his strength prove as unstable as water and he calleth understanding his mother, yet the utterance of lips is a superfluity, for mine is greater wisdom. Before he show his cunning I will smite him with the plague and humble him; his bones will I break."

Ere he was done speaking these words to himself he girded on his sword and issued forth from the forest, his mouth gaping wide. Upon his going out he found a wild ass, at home in the wilderness, and roared toward him; but the wild ass that confronted him was seeking an occasion against him and was not humbled by his roaring. In the eyes of the king this was astonishing, and he said: "Who is this that goeth, and turneth not back at my voice, but abideth before me? Is this the man, of whom my father spoke? Now shall I do that which is in my heart." And he came upon him and smote him, but the wild ass did not recognize him. Ere the lion withdrew his hand he spilled his liver to the ground, and ere he was dead he set about devouring him. Then the wild ass cried out: "Help me, King Lion, our lord. Where art thou and where thy goodness and loving-kindness to deliver thy servant from the hand of his smiter? He is a mighty warrior." And it came to pass when the lion heard him that he knew he had wounded him, and he said: "Who art thou that thou hast rebelled against me? Am I not King Lion, who walks with the eagle?" When the wild ass heard his words he fell before his feet and bowed down to him, for that he was his lord, and he said: "I the wild ass am thy servant; do thou spare me. I have sinned, for I recognized not the king and his roar." The king swathed his face, which was defiled with blood, and said: "Hast thou seen the son of man? What are his deeds and his ways? His expectation shall be shamed." Said the wild ass: "I know not. His voice have I not heard nor have I passed through his land nor have I come to the lodging where he lies, for I know not where it is. Never have I seen him, to know whether he be esteemed or contemptible. But do thou go hence and come to a plain where thou wilt find ass and ox; they know him for they have served him from of old. My words are finished in thine ears; understand well what is before thee." Thus far he spake, and the lion went upon his way.

He found a wild mule and an elephant and laid their lofty stature low. Thence he went forth to break breaches as he walked abroad in the land. And it came to pass as he issued forth from the forest that he saw a horse; strong was he, of handsome stature, clothed with high spirit, sleeker than perfumer's oil, swifter than lightning, and without blemish from his feet to his back. When the lion saw this spectacle envy burned within him, but the horse clothed him in awe for the day of wrath, saying: "Who is this man?" One called to the other, shouting bitterly with all their might, so that the earth was cleft by their voices. And when the lion approached near, the horse reared up on his legs to fall upon him and destroy him; but the lion nimbly leapt aside and escaped, so that the horse had no power over him. The lion took position to the rear of the horse, to harass him, himself being very wary. The horse in his great pride thrust backward, not forward, and clothed him with zeal as with a mantle. He waxed fat and kicked with his hind legs and smote the lion in his loins so that the blow descended even to his arms. When the lion saw that he had wounded him, he grasped his tail, and his wrath burned within him; he ran against the horse in fury and stretched out his right arm and requited his enemy to his face. Terror encompassed his fangs, and he crushed him like a bruised reed. Then did the hooves of the horse grow faint, and before he turned from his wrath the lion roared over his prey and tore at the horse's arm and even his head. The horse fell and knelt, doing obeisance upon his knees, and he cried out: "Help! Lo, I am thy servant, for thou art stronger than I; let thy breath not grow noisome." Said the lion; "Art thou man, whose might is great?" And he said: "Nay, I am horse, and there is none like me. But thou who art so strong, who art thou?" And he said: "I am lion. But where is man? If thy soul is weary of him, wherefore hast thou not smitten him to the ground?" And he said: "Prithee, my lord, I am my master's carrier, to do the desires of himself and all the people of his land." Said the king: "Where is he?" And he said: "Lo, he is in his field, gathering up his work. If it be to battle thou hast gone forth, go hence and thou wilt find him; lo, he is at his tilth; man abideth not in honor."

The lion came to the plain and saw the man binding sheaves to complete his work. And at his coming he saw the ass perishing and lying down under his burden, and the sheep were there also. Dread fell upon them, and they said: "Where is our master?" When the lion heard, he approached them and saluted them in peace. He asked them what their work was and who was their master. Said they: "We are slaves of the man who owns us, and each receives his rations from him. We know not what we shall do. Our soul loathes bread other than his. It is better for us to serve him than to be thy slaves." Said the lion: "Whither hath this great people gone?" Said they: "The man fared hence to the forest to hew wood; of his own rede doth he take counsel. His household hath ridden forth with him."

While they were yet conversing, lo, the fox approached, and the king was pleased to see him. Said he: "This one bringeth tidings; I shall not doubt them." When the fox reached him he knelt at his feet and said: "Is it peace with my lord?" And he answered, "Peace, my son." Said the fox: "I went forth and ambushed a bird's nest and its chicks; I left the winged folk no branch." The king answered and said: "And was not man on guard? Was he not there, or didst thou prove stronger than he?" Said the fox: "It was by lurking I took my prey, not by strength; for who am I and who my people?" Said the king: "Abide with me until I find him; surely I shall smite him in my wrath, a single stroke—I shall need no second. This place is a place of cattle; thou shalt graze in fat pastures." Said the fox: "So be it, my lord king, according to thy words; I shall follow after thee. But beware of snares; the man thou seekest thou shalt find in the thicket of the forest, for he has but now gone forth from his house. Thou shalt approach him to do battle with him and take much booty." So the lion walked with a high hand, and the fox remained in that place.

The parable: Beware of the wicked in every way, for sons do the deeds of their fathers, just as the lion who slew oxen and slaughtered sheep, whether by his nature or by his will.

107

Elephant & Hunter

THOUGH HIS BEGINNING BE STRAIT,
MUCH WILL HE ATTAIN IN HIS END.

THE ELEPHANT is remarkable among the beasts for his figure, his stature, and his aspect, for he is filled with bones and his tusks are encompassed with dread. His neck is two hundred cubits long and issues from his midst, from his breast, between his thighs; it ascertains the what and wherefore of things, and gathers his food into his mouth at a single sweep. It is a full wagon, laden with destruction. His rider is a city and its inhabitants. His maw gapes wide and ascends to his back; he is able to bear burdens, and his stride is exceeding broad.

An expert hunter of the field was tracking and hunting game when lo, an elephant with all his figure and stature and aspect came toward him. The man approached ever nearer, his sword girt upon his thigh. And it came to pass when the elephant came nigh him that he gnashed his teeth against him and opened his measureless maw and hurled him far off. The man was weary and fordone, and his hams touched one another as he walked; he desired to tar his dogs on to bite the elephant—blood is not atoned but by the blood of him that shed it. The man took thought against him: perhaps he could cast him down into his gin. He spread his snare and his ropes and made toils and snares in the forest and chased the elephant until he came thither, but the elephant broke and tore them and destroyed them utterly. Then he whetted his sword; perhaps he could do battle with him. And he went and attacked him and strove to slay him, seeking an opening against him. But when he lifted his hand against him and

201

gathered his strength, his sword was broken and crumbled like potter's ware.

When he saw that he could not prevail against him, he cried for all the people to assemble and said to them: "Mine is this elephant; I have desired him and cast my face upon him. By my cunning I have not availed to capture him in my net and snare, nor yet by my sword and bow; as I am bereft so am I bereft. Do ye pursue after him; perhaps ye will overtake him. When terror and trembling seize him ye will confound him and the mixed multitude which is in his midst; be ye zealous to master him." Quickly they cast him in their pit and captured him in their zeal and wrath and brought him to his master, the hunter of the field. His master said in his heart that he would lord it over him with hard labor and humble his heart with toil. He mounted upon his back and said to him: "Wherefore hast thou so done, to walk frowardly with me, in furious anger and rebelliousness? Me didst thou hurl behind thy back; therefore art thou encompassed with gins and snares."

When he saw that there was no stranger with him he wrapped his face in his cloak and rode upon the elephant until the setting of the sun. As the sickle was raised against the standing grain the reapers saw him and hid from him in the forests; the sinews of their stones were wrapped together in their fright, for they imagined that the demon had invaded their field. Each man said to his fellow: "We have seen the demon upon his horse." And they cried and wept all the night with the voice of great consternation, for lo, a dark dread had fallen upon them. Lamentation waxed strong among them, until they reached an inhabited city, and they said: "Bring forth every stranger and sojourner to make the demon flee from before us. Art thou for us or for our adversaries?" All the city was in tumult over them, and they said: "Against ghoulies and ghosties we shall not do battle, lest we become a laughing-stock and a disgrace." So they forsook their tents, their cattle and their asses, and men and women fled from that place. The man with the elephant came and found their tents as they had been left, filled with precious treasure, gold and silver, sheep and oxen. He sent and fetched them he loved, and summoned all his kinsmen, and he brought forth from the city every desirable thing, whether in chest or tower or press. Over the excellent sheep and oxen and fatted bulls, mother and children rejoiced; but the city was a desolate waste, without man or cattle, without sheep or its multitude of oxen. Even as the king had come upon it to waste it, so he came upon another city and did unto it as he had done to the first, which was left desolate; and so to the third and fourth, to the fifth, sixth, and seventh, and to the eighth and ninth; and so to the tenth also, wherein all he had ransacked was for devouring. And he returned to his house in peace and enriched. He informed them what his hire would be for exorcising the demon which had devastated the land, and they vowed to give him half his plunder, half to be returned to them. So did that man do, and they forgave him that which he had already done.

The parable is for a calculating and wise man who is ready to pursue after his provender. Every day is he weary and fordone, and he finds no respite for his soul nor gains aught by his toil, as befell that man who was alone with the elephant. But when the word of the king touches him so that his fortune waxes strong upon him and raises him ever higher, as when the master of the elephant was enlarged, he must keep his hand from rapine and theft and from the deeds he had wrought, as did that man with his booty. Like a lion he strengthened himself to return the half. If his beginning were strait, much did he attain in the end. Upon savory fare does he dine, and his righteousness stands forever.

108

Cat, Bird, Fox, Hare

A MAN FILLED WITH EVIL AND
PERVERSION CAUSES DISSENSION
AND BLOWS BETWEEN BRETHREN.

A CAT dwelt in the ruins of houses. From their windows sprouted wheat, of which a few grains were pecked by a bird. The cat thought to hold the bird fast, and said: "Wherefore is my soul straitened, while this bird hath much wheat and barley and liquors of banqueting and joy? Its days all pass without breach or plaint. I said of laughter, It is mad; my soul and my flesh are for a prey. At my soul's desire I shall eat flesh, and in famine I shall not lack food." So the cat went toward the bird privily; but the bird escaped from the spread snare and flew a short space away, lest it be a target for the arrow; it kept a distance of two bowshots. But the cat called to it and pleaded: "Why hast thou fled from me? If thou desire a wife such as I, spread thy wing over thy maidservant. I love the habitation of thy house; upon thee have I reposed my trust, and I have called thee unto me in love. Thou shalt rule my every limb. Come, my beloved, let us fare forth into the field. I shall trample and devour, and thou rend and rieve, and our prey we shall divide by lot together; better are two than one." But the bird made its reply: "Lo, the rains are over and gone, and the time of the singing of birds is come. I shall not alter or change my good wife for a bad. I will not add to her, nor from her diminish. Mine eye is single upon the life of my spouse, no less than hart and doe, and I shall enter no conspiracy. Speak to me no more." Answered the cat: "I am bereft and desolate; of me thou shalt not be afraid, for in my house have I brought thee persuasive gifts. Thou knowest not my lowliness, for I know and shall say after my death that the mouth of strange women is a deep pit." With her large discourse she inclined him to approach nearer, but for her it was confusion and shame, for as they were still conversing there came from the thickets of the forest a fox and a hare and they smote the cat unto death. The vulture escaped from all harm, for he was its enemy and had done no evil; but the cat who had thought to take its soul, her deed was requited upon her head, and it was done to her as she had schemed to do. Afflicted and tempest-tossed was she, and not comforted.

The parable is for a man filled with evil and perversity, who causes dissension and blows between brethren; he lays his friends and comrades low with gins and snares and the prancing of his mighty ones. You will find that it shall be done to him to the full as he had schemed to do to his fellow men.

109

Crab, Frogs, Crane

A RULER WHO HEARS LYING
WORDS INQUIRES AND SEARCHES
AND INVESTIGATES WELL.

A CRAB grew up in water. Out of his hands he had horns, he was all turned black, and he went not forward but backward. A frog stood at his side and croaked in his ear to frighten him. Said the crab: "What is this sound in my ears? Woe to all my neighbors for the noise of the ravaging host! I have heard and have aroused me to betake myself to the fish for refuge, lest the frog master us." Said the fish to him: "Gird the remnant of thy wrath to follow the counsel of the crane. His beak is narrow and sharp, and he eats frogs altogether; his neck is exceeding long; who can stand before him?" The crab came to the crane and said: "At my terror at the voice of the roaring of the frog my hair trembleth; I am the witness that knows. Prithee, my lord, hear me; have mercy upon me for I am cut off. Deliver me from this fury; enough of the thunder which the raging frogs croak in my ears with their gaping mouths." Answered the crane: "Lo, I dwell in the covert of reed and fens to cut off thence every creeping abomination. Whence hast thou come in thy bereavement? Tell me what my hire shall be and put thy price down in my hand, lest I swallow thee at a gulp." Said the crab: "I am hard and I am small. I am lacking in limbs and in fat and flesh; what savor canst thou find in me? In the day thou confrontest me, know what is before thee. Set thy face toward the frogs; put not a knife to thy throat. Of the frogs thou canst eat thy fill as thy soul desires." The crane answered in a soft voice: "There is none wise and understanding as thou. Thou shalt be over my house all the days of my life, until the day of my death." So the twain concluded a covenant against the frogs to cut them off from the marshes and the rivers and the seas. And the crab and the crane rested without fear—for not one frog was left—as brethren that dwell together. And from their enemies the frogs, who croaked aforetime, there was no utterance and no speech.

The parable is for a man full of wisdom, without deception or falsehood. Slanders that are framed against him are disdained along with them that walk in crooked ways. As a ruler who hears lying words inquires well and searches out and investigates, in order to abolish afflictions abroad, so shall he be diligent and vigilant lest from the granary and winepress, from his household and family and native place, they enlarge their stride against him. He shall do well in his actions and in his words, as he had done with his fathers, and he shall pay his neighbor his hire, upon that day or the morrow, as the crane requited the crab— and the name of his brother was Joktan.

110

Ant & Mouse

LIKE FIRE UPON A LEAFY TREE
IS THE FLAME OF SCORN
FOR THE BOLE OF THE CONFIDENT.

T HE ANT, not a strong folk, was scornful of the mouse. As she gathered her bread in summer she came to the edge of the heap at the beginning of barley harvest to glean among the sheaves; it was in compassion for her soul that she toiled, to prepare her food in harvest season. There she saw many mice making free of wheat and barley; six measures of barley they meted out to themselves to bring to their holes, until they had enough and to spare. The ant was filled with wrath and addressed them with contentious words and uttered stinging reproaches: "Wherefore have ye presumed to do so unto me? Have ye no fear of my furious indignation? I am the ant; I am a prince, for I have a garment. I am ruler and I am overseer; I remember injuries and avenge them. For me and over me, there is no king, of all the creeping creatures that walk upon the belly. Why have ye vexed me to take of my granary and my threshing?" Answered the mouse: "Mine is the granary and mine the grain. Wherefore hast thou slandered me? For me it was ruin. Surely thou art despised before me; how canst thou learn to do battle with me? Stay, arise out of the dust, awaken thee; dwell wherein thou dwellest; tread not the strength of my soul. I have eaten of my honeycomb and my honey, and my labor has sufficed for them. Who shall pass over the sea for us?" The ant returned her sayings; her strokes were from sea to sea. Her stings she dispatched against their nobles, against the mice according to their families and against their toil wherewith they toiled. In the days of snow they robbed their water. She returned to her companions to relate to them all that had befallen her, and she said: "I have labored and succeeded; I have tasted and eaten and been satisfied with bread and dainty viands upon the mountains of spices. But the evil mice, those wicked vermin, have reached to my very soul, so that I cannot lift my head. They have gleaned among the sheaves and the provender; the little foxes have spoiled our vineyard. Come ye forth with me to encounter them; I know their battle encampment." The ants hearkened to her, and with them came the cats, to be their auxiliaries and lurk for their blood in their coverts. They came to their place and there encamped until they had consumed them. The ants entered their holes and smote their soles with shoes and mounted upon the backs of the mice as do the bees. They stung them to the quick, to their very souls, until they came forth from their place. Then they brought forth the wheat and the barley and heaped it in heaps. The cats filled their belly with the mice and worked their will upon their enemies; and the ants, not a strong people, but one despised, destroyed them and dwelt in their place until this day.

The parable is for a man poor and humble by the side of a man rich and proud. The pauper speaks pleadingly with him, for he sues for his love, but the rich man answers sternly: "Who has heard the like?" He invents slanders against him to drive him from his livelihood, and his stench rises over him like a fire upon a leafy tree, a flame of scorn upon the thought of him that is at ease. His feet are ready for the appointed day. So is the rich man with his snares. Every driven leaf drives him forth, but God seeks out the driven.

And I plied my poesy and said in my response:
God judges the righteous;
He impoverishes the rich and the poor he enriches.

III

Spider, King, Slave

THOSE UPON WHOM THE RICH TAKE
NO MERCY ASCEND UPWARD,
WHILE THE RICH DESCEND
DOWNWARD TO THE PIT.

THE SPIDER is in the palaces of kings. Her hand holds the distaff, to weave and attach webs to level surfaces and to any beams of walls from houses and tents. The king built a house of great hailstones, but the spider made a web inside it to where the king sat at his table, and the king's anger burned within him. The servant approached, as was his way, to cleanse the house in its breadth and length, and he looked at the spider's web on the beams which went up to the four corners, east, north, west, and south, and he said to the spider: "We cannot dwell together, with the king and his servants. I shall sweep thee out with the besom of destruction." The spider proceeded to the wine and the water and the mead, to cast her poison into the liquors. And the man did not get off innocent; his belly swelled and his thigh rotted. The servant went weeping to his master to tell the tale of the accursed water turning bitter. The king commanded that the beverages be poured out in the streets and in the market places. The servant said: "A bitterness greater than death's do I pour forth." The matter was searched into, and it was found that when the sheep and the swine came from forest and field they drank of their mingled drink, and their bellies swelled and their thighs rotted of the liquor which had been poured forth. They drank and swilled it down, and were quenched like flax. Men sensed the thing which had befallen in the past: By means of a small insect a man big as a giant had been strangled—by draining the cup of poison for which there is no cure or remedy or relief. When the king saw this miracle his heart was jubilant, for he had been saved from great calamity, from a loathsome death to life; his life was in the balances before him. He made a banquet for all his friends, his household, and his kinsmen, and he said: "Better is it for me now to convert the spider from her evil."

So he came to her tent and commanded his servants to enjoin her to come at the king's bidding. Then he said: "I have established peace in thy boundary. I had dealt rebelliously with thee, I had decked my bed with coverings of tapestry were I not afraid of thy destruction and devastation. Now make broad the place of thy tent and the curtains of thy dwelling. Come and lodge where I lodge. How beautiful are thy feet with shoes! Lo, this house have I built thee to live in in return for the evil I did thee. Thou shalt no more sorrow forever, and no more shall evil or deception against thee enter my heart, for thou hast brought me so far as this and hast made my remembrance peace, if thus thou do to me and thine anger against me is abated." The spider answered with harsh words: "There is a time to speak and a time to be silent. Thou hast driven me out from abiding in thine inheritance; lo, I shall send against thee and thy houses a heavy plague of flies. Thou shalt not avail to stand before me, nor yet to be healed, for thou wilt be destroyed by death." And she went and collected all the spiders from houses and valleys, and they all gathered together to attack the king and his servants, and they assailed them to confound and destroy the men until they were consumed. They set watchers and taskmasters over them, and when deep sleep fell upon the men they fell and died in multitudes and not one was left.

The parable is for the poor and needy, upon whom the rich take no mercy, but instigate others to injure them, as though they had been their enemies from of old. But the poor take thought for their latter day and make bands against their death and shrewdly take vengeance to requite them for their treacherous dealing against them. They become pricks in their eyes and thorns in their sides, until they come and kneel and prostrate themselves at their feet to forgive their transgression and remit their sins. And they are humbled and return to the heel of their shame, and they descend lower and lower, down to the pit; and the poor ascend higher and higher. And Solomon in his wisdom hath said:"There is one that maketh himself poor yet hath great riches, but he turns his ear aside from hearing the poor man when he cries."

112

Man, Rock, Mouse

MEN WHO CANNOT ATTAIN FIRM
TRUTH WEAVE A SPIDER'S WEB.

THERE was a man who boasted of his shrewdness
and cunning and ingenuity and declared that with
his blade he could impregnate the great rock which was
in the wilderness and within a month without deception
bring to birth and release a living creature. The people of
the place went astray after him and hearkened to wizards
and magicians. The man kept a big mouse, and at the
season he appointed he placed the mouse in a crevice of
the rock, where it was held prisoner until the folk came
there. The cracks of the rock the man stopped up, and he
went and gathered the folk, saying: "Hasten, come ye
after me and I will fulfill my saying." Those that doubted,
together with those that believed, journeyed forth as one
man, and said with mocking lips: "Who hath heard such
a thing, who hath seen such a thing? Shall earth travail
and a mountain bring forth? But this man hasteneth to
verify his word." The man who boasted of his handiwork
took in his hand a staff, which he raised against the rock,
and he said: "Hear ye, my masters; shall I bring forth a
living creature out of the rock and produce it before you?"
And he smote the rock with his staff to cast down from it
all that he had placed over the opening, and the mouse
emerged, all black. Said he: "The mouse was born, and
lo, he hath come forth; of all my words none hath fallen
to the ground."

The parable is for those who hearken to falsehood and
walk in darkness. They believe in words of those who

daub with untempered mortar and work in miry clay.
They conceive mischief and bring forth iniquity. They
put their trust in falsehood and vanity. Any who joins
them shall be even as they. Those that play the harlot after
them, away from the path of the sensible and the seemly,
vanity are they and the work of errors. For that they do
not attain the right they weave spider's webs. But their
wiles cannot serve for a garment, nor can they clothe
themselves in their deeds. They think to lead people astray
by their devices, by their visions and falsehoods and shak-
ings; but foolish indeed are they, for they stumble in the
snare of their folly. Help they cannot, nor can they deliver.

113

Man & Wolf

A MAN WHOSE EYE AND HEART
ARE BENT ON GAIN, HIS MOUTH
DECLARES HIS WICKEDNESS.

A MAN taught the letters of the alphabet to a wolf. He
said to him, "Say *aleph*," and the wolf answered,
"Aleph." Then he said, "Pray say *beth*," and the wolf
guarded the utterance of his lips and said *beth* and *gimel*
after him. Said the man: "Now listen to what I set before
thee, so that thou mayst recognize the letters and put them
together and so be able to pronounce what thou wilt.
When thou combinest the letters together, we shall be one
people. Put *aleph* and *beth* together as I do." The wolf responded "Sheep!"

The parable is for one whose eye and heart are bent

upon gain. His mouth will declare his wickedness and his lips will testify against him to reveal the frowardness of his heart. Wickedness will issue from his belly when evil is found in his mouth, and his thoughts can be recognized from his deeds. He despises Jacob and chooses Esau. His righteousness goeth before the righteous but the perverseness of transgressors shall destroy them. Solomon's proverb [Proverbs 14.22] retains its force. "They that devise evil go astray."

114

Chameleon & Merchants

HE WHO IS FILLED WITH TAINT
AND ABOMINATION AND FRIVOLITY
IS ACCOUNTED BY MEN AS UTTERLY VILE.

A CHAMELEON rooted with her teeth after the roots
and shrubs which were under her feet. She threw
the dirt over her as she went hither and yon to spread her
rooting, and the field was filled with many mounds. There
came thither merchants to seek roots for medicines, and
they searched for them until the chameleon came out of
her place toward them. Said they: "Upon the testimony
of two witnesses shall the culprit be put to death"—and
they pursued her as far as the mound. Into the mound the
chameleon escaped, and she laughed at them and called
out: "Why have ye chased after me? I know my house,
wherein I may hide to deliver my soul from death and
keep me alive in famine. I shall walk in the land of the
living and shall not be for a laughingstock. Never again
shall ye see me. The roots which ye are seeking, I have
uprooted all, for in my heart is the day of vengeance. Ye
shall return empty-handed, shamed and discomfited and
disgraced among the physicians and among the people.
Healers of vanity are ye all, with your charlatanry and
your wiles. Depart from me quickly; let not the light of
day shine upon you. Everyone will whistle at you, and I
shall not spare you my spittle. Baser and viler are ye than
all men who have exchanged their honor for shame." The
men turned away thence to seek roots in another place,
and the chameleon sent her daughter after them to carry
out her devices and uproot the roots from the earth. Said
she: "Whoso breaches a wall, may a serpent bite him;

these men menace our lives by taking provender and sustenance for their souls from us." The daughter went according to her counsel and did all that her mother commanded her. She came to the place of their sojourn and returned not until she had destroyed all the roots in the ground. She destroyed them forever, so that not one root was found. The men went from that place together, and the chameleon ran after them to tell them that she had done this thing. Said she: "Wherefore have ye toiled for vanity? Who is he and where is he that durst presume in his heart to do so? There is not a wise man among you. I am blind and ye have eyes, yet from me do ye take spices and medicaments. Mine is counsel and wisdom to recognize all the roots of the earth, which of them are good for plaisters, and also all species of dye—white, red, green, and black. But ye walk backward; day and night ye weary yourselves, but find no root." The men did not know at all where her place was under the ground, for the battle is not to the strong nor the race to the swift to reach their goal. These men came to the camp, but there was none to heed their voice and none to answer.

The parable is for a man who boasts of his great wisdom, of his beauty and comeliness and stature, saying there is none like him on earth—who is he and where is he? His heart is emptier of understanding than all men of good faith, but he is filled with taint and abomination and frivolity and folly and is accounted among men as the exaltation of the vile. Out of his vaunted wisdom he will go bowed down; instead of wheat there will come forth a thorn. In all labor there is profit and smoothness, but the talk of the lips tendeth only to penury. And the Preacher hath said in the proverbs of prophecy [Proverbs 17.10]: "A reproof entereth more into a wise man than a hundred stripes into a fool."

115

An Old Man & His Sons,
a Captain & His Men

HE WHO HONORETH HIS FATHER

EVEN IN DRINKING, HIS

REWARD WILL NOT BE FALSE.

THERE was a man in the land, old and richer than any
creature; his wealth extended everywhere, and his
sons were with him in his house. He called to them to
declare his will: "Hear, my sons, the commandment of
your father, for I am old and know not the day of my
death. Pray, give ear to me, ye princes, and hear whether
my words be just. Hearken to me, my sons all: I have
money in my treasuries; take it all for yourselves and
divide it among you. Leave not anything with me, but
only give me wine from year to year." The old man finished his injunctions, and his sons did for him as he had
said. Every day they found wine for him, until after many
years they grew weary. They took counsel among themselves and made their father drunk with white wine and
red, until he fell asleep before them. Then they summoned
their neighbors and said: "Come ye hither, ye that pursue
after rewards, and see what hath befallen us; for our in-
iquities our father hath died." And they went and wept
for him and performed the customary usages. The sons
dressed him in shrouds and carried him to a cave which he
had got ready. And it came to pass that a captain came
upon that day; his retinue was large, and there was the
noise of a multitude. They sat them in the cave by companies and began to eat and drink. The man awoke from
his wine and arose to go to his home; the feasters saw him

from afar and left off their eating. The captain said to them: "Truly, this man is dead." The men arose in great fear and departed and left all their possessions; and when the sons came to the cave to see him they found great wealth with him. There they rejoiced mightily, and the favored people went to their house.

The parable is for a man who fills his belly and bowels with dainties, and to the drinker gives wine.

116

An Old Man, His Son, a Fish, the Leviathan

HE WHO DOES THE COMMANDMENT
OF HIS FATHER, EVEN THE
LEVIATHAN WILL FORGIVE HIS SIN.

THERE was an old man devout and humble whose eyes had grown heavy with age. He put his trust in the Rock who created him. As he lay sick upon his bed he yearned for his elder son, and in view of his approaching death commanded him: "Cast thy bread upon the waters, for thou shalt find it after many days." And it came to pass after the old man died that the son sat upon his father's chair and did as he had commanded him; he walked in the way his begetter had led him and cast his bread into the sea without stint. God caused a great fish to eat his bread until he was satisfied. One greater than his neighbor swallowed him; the great fish proclaimed a day of slaughter for the fish round about, and in sorrow they went to the Leviathan, who was chief of them that handle the oar. The great fish trod his bow in strength against the fish; he wrought destruction among them without mercy and cut their branches off. The Leviathan commanded that he be summoned: "Let him not stand, though his host be great, lest the glory of his nostrils lose their terror. I shall slay him in battle." The great fish came bellowing and lamenting and storming mightily because of his strength; with a great trembling did that fish tremble, for he seethed in his depths like a pot. The Leviathan kindled his anger against him and his eyeballs gleamed like the dawn. Said he: "How couldst thou presume, how could thy heart embolden thee, to do such a thing? Who hath made thee ruler and judge over us? Art thou the man who hath consumed us?" The great fish drew near and confessed: "Let not thine anger kindle if I tell thee the truth. I did in mine iniquity murder, and this thing and that have I done." The Leviathan answered: "From whose hand hadst thou thy repast, who hath fed thee to this point?" And he said: "There is a man whose way it was to sustain me with daily rations; in truth he is responsible for his own injury." Answered the Leviathan: "If thou wouldst atone thy sin, violate not my commandment. Go thou to thy haunt, where thou hast affirmed the man's habit of casting his bread to thee; when he seeks thee do thou swallow him, but keep his soul alive. Thereby wilt thou save thy life, for that thou hast slain without mercy." All answered, "This is appropriate," and the thing was determined and the great fish did so. He swallowed the man within his gullet and spewed him forth before his master. The Leviathan asked the man in anger: "What is this and why is this and wherefore hast thou given the fish thy food? It is not for thee to maintain him; but if it be so and thou art obliged to keep him, then must thou be destroyed for his sin." The man prostrated himself before him and said that he had done this thing in the innocence of his hands and by the commandment of his father. The Leviathan raised his hands and swore by his life that no hair of his head should fall: "Thou shalt not be judged by analogy, for thou hast kept a commandment, and art not responsible for its anomalous outcome. Open thy mouth and I shall fill it with the spirit of wisdom. Thou shalt be clever in all things and wiser than Darda and Chalcol." The saying of Leviathan was established; he was brought out from the sea, and his coming forth was very swift; none was found so wise as he. His history is duly recorded in a book of chronicles.

II7

Wolf & Fox

ALREADY HATH SOLOMON IN HIS
WISDOM SAID [PROVERBS 11.8]:
"THE RIGHTEOUS IS DELIVERED OUT
OF TROUBLE AND THE WICKED
COMETH IN HIS STEAD."

A FOX went strolling by a fountain and saw the shadow of the moon cast upon the water. He thought in his heart that it was a cheese and greatly desired to eat of it. There before him were buckets hanging in balance, and he looked at them with his two eyes. He put forth his hand and grasped the cords to divide the cheese into portions. As he entered one of the buckets he went down with it into the water; he cried a great and bitter cry and waited there for some man to come and help him. There came to the fountain a wolf, who saw the fox lurking there. Said the wolf: "What art thou doing there? Tell me what mark that is in the water." The fox answered and said: "I have eaten much cheese and am sated; more I could not eat. Some I have stored away for thee. Come hither now, as I advise thee, and eat it, and we shall be comrades together; better are two than one." The wolf hearkened to his counsel and said in his heart: "I will go with him." He put his hand to the bucket which was near him and grasped it and nimbly sate himself within it. Quickly he descended to the fountain, and by the pressure of his weight the fox ascended. The wolf opened his mouth to the shadow to swallow it, but saw that he could not. Said the fox: "By the life of my head, thou shalt not eat of it." The wolf seized the cord in his hand to pull it, but saw that all was vanity. He lifted his voice to the fox in lamentation and said: "Wherefore hast thou dealt treacherously with me?" The fox answered him: "Let be; the wicked cometh in place of the righteous. For such a case hath Solomon in his wisdom said: 'The righteous is delivered out of trouble and the wicked cometh in his stead'."

One day the man went to the fountain, and with him were his wife and daughter and son. The maiden came after them slowly, with her pitcher resting upon her shoulder. In this manner they all went onward until they stood by the fountain. The man drew up the bucket, which showed him the wolf. Said he: "From the water have I drawn him forth." All looked upon the wolf, and the man desired to smite him. All surrounded him and began to beat him with their sticks, until they were wearied. The wolf ran, and they all came after him and pursued him to the place of his dwelling. Then they all returned to the fountain to draw water for their need. The maiden hastened and filled her pitcher and took it in her hand; then the girl lifted the pitcher and returned it to her shoulder, and they went and came to their house, and there they rejoiced with their fathers.

118

Youth, Rogues, Woman, Judge

WHOSO IN HATRED SEEKS A ROD
FOR THE BACK OF HIS BROTHER
WILL BE DESPISED FOR HIS ROD
AND CLOTHED IN SHAME.

A TRAVELER who could make music on any instrument came to a rich man. The rich man was handsome of figure, as though designed with compasses. His stature and the length of his limbs made him handsome; his fathers had exalted him as one chosen among the people. He asked the traveler: "Whence comest thou and whither goest?" And he said: "I come from a distant land. I have seen nobles riding upon horses. The land was good in my eyes; its merchandise is better than the merchandise of silver; and there is no lack of silver in it." Said he to him: "What is the city and what its name, from the time thou wert there?" Said he to him: "It is beyond Aram of the two rivers; it is Alexandria of Egypt." Said he: "So have I heard men say. I shall gather me comrades and go thither for trade, with cloth of goats and precious stones and with colored garments dyed in scarlet. I shall go to Egypt by boat upon the sea, with scarlet and purple and vesture and precious vessels of weight beyond calculation." He prepared all things, omitting none, and when the rainy season was past, he loaded his ship until it was full and overflowing and put in it shield and spear and armor. The sailors put out to sea and were carried forward by an east wind and made land, happy and joyful. They came before Alexandria, and the city was astonished at the sight of a mighty caravel, unparalleled for majesty at the haven of sea or the haven of ships; compared to it, all strength was trivial.

The young man disembarked from the ship and took a mule richly accoutred with bit and bridle, which he found in it, and rode to find entertainment. His report went forth in the streets and marketplaces, and certain rogues foregathered and formed a conspiracy to inspect the ship and its riches for the sake of combining against the young man to assault and fall upon him, and to seek a pretext and plot against him, for they were men of guile. The young man went hither and yon to see the city and the region, and a passerby encountered him and said: "To me shalt thou come. The Rock hath caused thee to meet with me, for we are both men of merchandise. If thou wilt, I shall buy all thy goods, for I have ships of Tarshish as well as lighter craft." The young man answered: "If thou hast leisure I shall gladly sell thee all. If it is thy will to purchase, what wilt thou give of all that is in the ship?" And he said: "As thou sayest and as thou choosest; I will fill thy vessel with goods of all sorts." And he said: "As thou sayest; the ship is before you; draw from it and make your purchase." So he bought the merchandise from him, and they separated, each man to his own house.

And it came to pass early on the morrow that he went to see his ship, and a man before him looked upon him, at the girdle upon his loins and the sword at his side girt over his garment. The man said: "Turn aside to me, turn aside, for the sword which is in thy girdle thou hast stolen from me, and also all my money." And he cited him to court to testify before the judge on an appointed day. The young man was meek, and he looked and his face fell. And it came to pass on the third day when it was morning that the young man arose to seek some helper. There met him a solitary man who was maimed; his right eye was gouged out. The man seized him and held him fast, so that he panted within him, and he said, "Why hast thou taken hold of me?"—"Because thou hast robbed mine eye; I will wager my soul against thine that that is mine eye which is in thy head." He found a guarantor for the judge, to be prepared for the day of strife, that he favor not the face of the poor but commit them to judgment. The law of the judge must be upright; he must not have respect to the rich. The man went upon his way, and the young man went on his way, weeping.

And as he went on in search of mercy there found him an old woman and said to him: "Why is thy face, which is handsome, sad?" He told her all that had befallen him and begged her to teach him what to do. Said she: "I shall not inquire or investigate but reveal their secret to you. All their glory and excellence is by the instruction of a very wise old man. With him they share all the profit they gain. They consult with him a day before their appointment and recount to him all their discussion and he writes their words down. They are afraid lest he tell their opponents, and they have nought to answer, and so they share their possessions with him. The old man lives in an upper chamber, and I in the house beneath. By the mercies of the Rock I will place thee at the crevice in the fortress and hide thee from them, and thou wilt hear all their words. And it came to pass on the day they came to take counsel that she hid him in the flax of the wood. They revealed to the old man the secrets of their houses and he considered them and determined the men to evil. The young man heard what was said and gave ear to the old man's speech, and his heart was cheered. They said: "Our lord is understanding and wise, but that young man is a fool and hath no wisdom." They went then to their house, and knew not that the interpreter had been between them.

Upon the day appointed they came to stand in judgment, and there were assembled smiths and hewers of wood and workmen of all kinds to make the day a blessing for the young man and deliver him and reward him for his deeds. Said the judge: "Let all who have suits stand and state their case." The first merchant whetted his tongue with pride: "Make thy demands great and I will give them; I will fill thy ship with all thou wilt say." The young man answered and said: "I desire of thee nought of gold and silver and broidered garments, nor perfumed essences of rich aroma; only fleas do I pursue; my request and my petition is that you fill my ship with them." Every man looked staring at his brother and said: "Hath a man so understanding as this been found?"

Then the second arose and said: "My lord judge, prithee hear: In my house I was quiet and serene from what I gathered and gleaned until I accumulated great wealth. This man came to my house and lay in wait and stole and took all for himself, even the sword which is upon him, and silver and gold and dyed garments. I call to testify against him faithful witnesses who identify the sword. Determine his penalty and sentence him. Let him pay me from his house, and if he have not wherewithal let him be sold for his theft." Then the young man arose before the judge and said: "My lord, I come from the land of Canaan and from France and Spain. In all this my heart hath not trembled nor hath my way been perverse, until I came to the land of Ararat. From there I went to Ispahan, and now am I come to Alexandria to display the sword and see whether a man can be found who will be willing to recognize and acknowledge it. Blessed be the Rock and his mindfulness, for he hath prospered my way. I have labored, and I have succeeded. Lo, with this sword was my father slain, to my great sorrow, and it was found stuck in his belly. My lord judge, here he is in thy hand; do but keep his soul until I ride upon the ass and bring witnesses to the matter; it shall not be forgotten."

Then the third rose in anger, panting to slay the young man, and he spoke against him proud words which were astonishing in the eyes of all: "My lord, this is the man who came to rend me like a lion, and he surpassed me in strength and gouged out my right eye and by his magic and wizardry put my eye in his head. And now if he do

not confess I will prevail over him with hard labor. I shall
do battle against him and overcome him. I shall sling a
stone into his forehead. Do determine my case; let him
indemnify me for my eye and for my pain and medical
fees and unemployment and incapacitation, for it was in
violence that he came against me." Said the young man to
the judge: "Prithee, my lord, thou knowest that I am
from a distant land and remote from father and brother
and sons. Hear if my words be just, if the law of my land
is upright and approved in thy sight. Gouge out that man's
left eye and also my right eye which he claims was his.
Put the two eyes in scales; if they balance and are equal,
then is his claim correct. But if one outweighs the other,
then shall they see to it that judgment be executed upon
him in the view of all, in the vale of Jehoshaphat. With
me he shall not fight, but if he confesses and forsakes his
evil he shall be pardoned." And so the deceivers were de-
feated and remained vanquished. They gave the young
man all their wealth, and their strength and might were
forsaken.

This my parable is an allegory of a man filled with
  iniquity and deception,
Who sought to injure the innocent by working guile
  and fraud.
His day of retribution will come, and his measure
  will be very full;
Into the pit he delved and dug, will he fall in
  trembling and consternation.
There is a man who seeks a rod for his brother's
  back in frowardness and hatred,
But a time will come when he is despised with his
  rod and swathed in shame.
There is a man who breaches his neighbor's hedges
  for reproachful deeds and devastation,
But there will come a day when the serpent will bite
  him and exact vengeance.

Attend to this my parable, ye sons of man, and
multiply not vanity and guilt
As did the three in the story; but they were overturned and left empty-handed.

Go, my parables, to a man whose understanding
Perceives that my words are true and upright,
To be collected with those tested and tried.
If ye have truly found favor in his eyes and no
recrimination,
Then shall I pray the Blessed to make you lie down
in mansions.
Similarly, if he find and point any frowardness in you,
I pray he will hide your manuscript away,
That the memorial of iniquity be nevermore seen.

119
The Envious Man & the Covetous

THE COVETOUS AND THE ENVIOUS
TOGETHER WILL BE CLOTHED
IN CONFUSION, AND IN THE END
BOTH WILL BE MULCTED ALIKE.

HEAR ye the matter of Rabbi Crispia ha-Nakdan, who
did judge the heart of an envious man and a covetous and adjudged them to sword, slaughter, annihilation,
and the corruption of eternal loathing, and thereby subdued and humbled him who would subvert weight and
measure and whose wrath was kindled at the strength of
justice and the force of the decree. So hath it befallen man

—aye, men froward and passionate, one covetous and the other envious.

Each hated his brother, and they uttered many recriminations against their Creator, who knoweth the evil of their inclinations, and wickedly they murmured against him. The covetous man would speak as follows: "See how evil and bitter are all the works of God! He has brought the lofty low; why am I poor and indigent, whereas that man, mine enemy and neighbor that dwelleth at my right hand, is rich? He resteth under his standard; why doth he lift his foot to horse and chariot? My soul longs and yearns for his lot, for it is wholly desirable, and my heart turns toward him, to rest in his place." Said the envious man with his wonted hatred: "God will not turn toward thee nor hearken to thy voice to make thee a prince over people. Let me die if thou grow rich or if thou avail to be as I am, clothed in scarlet. I say to God, Make me not guilty. Who can hasten more than I, or who live? I would not that all sons of man possess wealth; enough for thee the livelihood of flesh and blood. I shall walk alone all the days of my world in my riches and my glory, for my hand hath found might. If the time come when I am poor and needy, let my neighbor be even poorer, and all they that pass before me, that they be as grasshoppers in my eyes and all walk in darkness."

And it came to pass as they were walking and talking as they walked that the wrath of the speaker who wished to make a name for himself kindled; he was knowingly sinful. An angel of God found them in the wilderness of Leshem, and when the angel saw them he called to them and said: "What have ye seen and what have ye sought and what have ye inquired of passersby? Know ye your Creator?" And they said: "We know but shall not speak of him, for his doing is strange, so that none can abide it. To my neighbor hath he given all that mine eye desires, and me he hath made to lack all things. His kindness hath he removed from me until my soul is oppressed with

much jealousy and vexation, which beseemeth me not."
Such was the response of the covetous man in his singular
folly. May the form of the envious man's envy, the object
of his desire, never come about: "If a man as rich as I shine
forth at my side, better for me then is death than life, and
rotting of bones for envy. If thou heedest his prayer and
he ascend upward then shall I ascribe folly to God, and
slander rather than praise him." So they quarreled together
and emptied their sacks. Said the angel: "Be silent and
wait for your deliverance. Surely ye will be ashamed of
speaking against your Creator. Why do ye all quarrel
with me? Lo, I am sent before you to give each of you this
day his request and fulfill his petition. He is adequate to
your demands. The Almighty will vouchsafe you your
deserts; raise not your contention against me. He will
speak, and it shall come to pass. Suddenly it will come
upon you, with strength greater than any people. This is
what I grant you: One of you two shall have whatever
his mouth utters; it shall come upon him in an instant.
And a double portion of what he asks shall accrue to his
fellow, who is last in order. This shall be the covenant
which ye must not violate. Pass ye over and go upon your
way; all that ye shall choose shall come to pass for you."
They hearkened to him and said: "Lo, we are thy servants,
and thou shalt be our lord; be thy loving-kindness upon
us, for we have repented."

And it came to pass as they spoke their words that the
angel departed from them, for the spirit bore him off; no
eye saw him, nor were his footsteps perceived. Then did
they understand and perceive that he was an angel of the
Lord and that the law of truth was upon his lips. Spake
the covetous one, who lusted for a double portion because
his uncleanliness was in his skirts, and said: "Do thou ask."
And the envious one answered him: "How shall I ask for
a thing when thou wilt emerge stronger than I and double
thy dominion and take the share of the firstborn? Thou
art the last, and therefore the profit will be thine and the

loss, mine. I come first, and how can I request some good thing which will make thy lot better and broaden thy boundaries? Is this a just sentence?" Said the covetous man to the envious: "Art thou envious of me? Make thy request deep or raise it so high that thou wilt have nought to lack and wilt not be taken away from being a city; why shouldst thou be envious when thy soul is filled with all good things? Thine expectations are realized, and thou canst put them in thy basket." Answered the envious man: "If it is truth thou speakest, do thou ask first, in accordance with thy logic, and I will come after thee. Do not thou lust for a double portion. I shall not stand, I shall not avail to lift my head, my soul shall choose strangulation, if thou make thy portion greater than mine, if thou be the last in order." The covetous man grew wroth in his heart and his anger burned within him. He turned upon the envious man in fury and smote him with a high hand; with stone and fist and with the staff in his hand, he belabored his back, and he said: "Ask thou straightway, and my redemption shall come after thee. If not I will destroy thee and slay thee forthwith." And it came to pass when the envious man saw that his hope was lost, that he still clung to his uncleanliness. Since he could no longer hope to make the other ask first he made oppression his level and crying his plumb; he trepanned his skull and battered his head, beating and bruising it. When the envious man's might prevailed, the covetous man was in straits and implored and supplicated him, saying: "My lord, let go of me; I shall ask first and do thou receive a double portion in the end, that there may be peace between us." So he let him go, yet did not release him wholly but held him by his skirts, lest he seek an occasion to flee hither or yonder.

Then spake the envious man, saying: "Prithee, Lord, do unto thy servant the reverse of thy kindness, to requite his deeds upon him. Blind me of one of my two eyes, but mine enemy, of both. Make one of my hands to fall, and double this measure for mine enemy." And it came to pass as he was thus speaking that an awful darkness fell upon them and smote them both with blindness. The profit of the second exceeded the weight of the first, so that he had double his fellow's measure; his words were fulfilled. He turned his face to his fellow, and lo, both his eyes were darkened and his two hands remained in the skirt of his garment, so that his strength departed from him. And lo, his two feet were cut off. And so the two remained there, for shame and disgrace. Their lust was removed from them and also their hatred, for the covetous man desisted from his covetousness; he was content with his livelihood and did not malign his wealth, nor any more covet the possessions of a lordly house, but only the grave. For now he could not avail to put food into his mouth, but only to lick up porridge, as an ox licks grass. Want of eyes resulted in bareness of teeth, nor could he perceive the goodliness of taste. Nor did he stir from his place; his feeding and evacuation were in the same spot, so that he was reckoned as an animal; better for him death than such confusion.

Nor did the envious man who hated his brother any longer begrudge others. His envy had departed at the ends of the members he had lost in his willfulness and had forfeited in his envy; he was smitten to destruction. For this hath Wisdom made her proverb, saying of the envious man [Proverbs 26.24]: "He that hateth dissembleth with his lips and layeth up deceit within him"—and poureth wrath over him. But justice observes measure, and thus it befell the man that was covetous. Covetousness closes the Ten Commandments, and envy closes the Song of Songs, which calls it cruel as the grave. It hath no redeemer to redeem it nor any good at all save envy of wisdom—envy of the works of the pious, not of the works of sinners. It is only wicked, not good. Out of envy cometh covetousness, for envy comes first, but its end is bitter as wormwood. Bitter will be the covetousness which ensues, for its rise is inevitable. It is all a single malady; the leprosy blooms and waxes great until it is sovereign and draws the heart of man to within the veil. In the end it will cast him down and abandon him in the field in disgust. For that he envies the money of others, his friends will dig a pit to snare him. Such is the judgment of the envious; surely whom God hateth, I hold in abhorrence.

Crispia ha-Nakdan petitions his Creator to guard him from envy and deliver him from covetousness. And him who transcribes Crispia's work may the Lord shield from covetousness and envy, from the pit and from hatred, and may no evil thing befall him. Let him not covet the wealth of others, among the youthful; and in old age let him not envy his neighbors their money and property but only their wisdom and their contemplation and their good deeds, which stand forever—to observe them and do as they do. They that do their deeds are like unto them. Envy like this is filled with all goodness, and so said the prophets [Proverbs 23.17]: "Let not thy heart envy sinners, but be thou in fear of the Lord"—and in the words of Mount Sinai, and in the zeal for retribution. He that giveth peace in his high places and in his innocent sheep Israel which is sealed with the eternal covenant, the Rock, whose name is forever, He will bless his people Israel with peace.

AMEN.

232

Done—praised be the Sovereign!—are the parables of
    Berechiah,
His proverbs are his allegories.
Wisdom he gathereth like gold and silver,
Folly he heweth apart and its lovers rejects.
His poesy strengthens the meek, abases the proud,
And causes haughty heads to stumble.
Pure sayings he gathers like herbs,
Bestows them in pots, readies them for cooking;
The wise esteem them as the chiefest spices,
Though to scorners and evildoers they are but broom.

    Ended are all the parables,
    Praised be the King of all the world.